SOLO

A DOWN TO EARTH GUIDE FOR TRAVELING THE WORLD ALONE

AARON HODGES

Edited by Genevieve Lerner
Proofread by Sara Houston
Cover by MIBLART

Copyright © December 2019 Aaron Hodges.
First Edition. All rights reserved.
ISBN-13: 978-0-9951296-58

CHAPTER ONE

AN INTRODUCTION OF SORTS

Oof, okay, I'll say it now. Introductions are the worst. And if I'm honest, writing in the first person, about myself (or at least my own thoughts and recommendations) is not something I'm used to. I mean, I *write*, it's just, my fiction books are generally just a tad...different. You know, dragons and magic and all that jazz.

Oh well, I'll do my best to make this bearable.

So, if you're anything like me when I first made the decision to put the brakes on my career and jet off on an adventure, you're probably sitting at your desk in the office, bored out of your mind. Hopefully your boss isn't reading this over your shoulder —although on the bright side, then you wouldn't have to *quit*, right? Anyway, what I'm getting at is...you're not happy, right? You wake up every day to your alarm, eat breakfast and head off to work, sit behind your desk until the numbers make sense, finish up and head to the gym, hopefully see some friends or loved ones, go to bed…only to get up and do it all again the next day.

And while you're doing all that, you're scrolling through Instagram or Facebook (or whatever social media platform the kids are using these days), seeing all these amazing adventures people are having. Your friend from high school is in Thailand jumping off waterfalls, that guy from your university group project is skydiving in New Zealand, your ex-girlfriend is kissing another guy in Paris.

Youch.

No wonder you want to get out of there.

Of course, the only problem is finding someone to join you. We've already established the ex ain't an option, and all your friends are busy finishing their university degrees, or starting new jobs, or entering relationships. I guess you'll just have to wait…

And wait.

And wait.

Yeah, exactly.

Don't wait, because take it from me, if you wait it's not going to happen.

Stop waiting, come and join me on an adventure

I'm going to let you in on a little secret. If you're reading this book, if you picked it up because you're alone, because you're hurt, because you're bored or feeling lost, you're the exact person I wrote this travel guide for.

Because at this moment in your life, you're free. There's no one to tell you "no," no responsibilities holding you back, nothing to stop you.

Now is the *perfect* time to have an adventure.

So let me be the first to welcome you to the world of the solo traveller.

CHAPTER TWO

WHY OH WHY?

Okay, now that the introduction is over, I should probably introduce myself and explain what this book is all about, right? My name is Aaron Hodges and I hail from New Zealand, a tiny country at the bottom of the world that's known for its sheep, rugby, and...umm, what was it? Oh yeah—*The Lord of the Rings*! I left home on my first solo trip way back in 2014, and have been travelling on and off ever since (5 years and counting at the time this book was published).

So if you stick around, hopefully I can impart at least a little bit of what I've learnt over that time. Or at least share a few tales of the adventures (and disasters) I've had along the way. There'll be plenty of tips about all aspects of solo travel and why I love it—but also an exploration of the pitfalls and downsides that go with it.

One thing this book *won't* be though is the written version of a travel influencer's Instagram feed. Yes, travel is amazing and exciting and potentially life-changing—but it can also be lonely, exhausting, boring, uncomfortable, and even dangerous at times (although hey, I'm still here so it can't be that bad, right?) As much as I love this new life I've discovered, I'm not going to shy away from the dark stuff.

Let's jump right into it then, shall we?

I'm going to assume you're single. WHAT? Why's that, you ask? Well, you are reading a book titled *SOLO*…right?

Okay, let me make a second wild guess, one based on something I've observed over the last few years on the road.

You recently went through a breakup.

Maybe I'm right, maybe I'm wrong, but one trend I've noticed over the years is that most new solo travellers needed a push to get them off the straight and narrow, and onto a new path. For many, that push seems to be the ending of a significant relationship. Not everyone of course. For others it might a feeling of unfulfillment in their career, or the realisation they've reached a crossroads in their life and aren't sure what direction to take next.

For myself, I had a little of each, but if I'm honest with myself, it was the breakup that put me over the edge.

At the end of 2013, my girlfriend of three years and I separated (okay, I was dumped), which left me in a pretty bad place. Suddenly I found myself heartbroken and alone, working in a job I did not enjoy, living in a city I hated. The following six months were pretty rough, as I struggled to restore myself to some semblance of normality.

I searched for a new job, I took up different hobbies, I dated. But nothing really changed, nothing moved me forward.

Pictured: The crushing weight of heartbreak.

Until I stumbled onto a company that advertised adventure travel for solo travellers. Suddenly I found myself wondering—could I really go off and see the world by myself? My girlfriend and I had been planning what we in New Zealand call an Overseas Experience (OE)—a long term trip around the world. But I had never really considered going it alone.

How would that even work?

I thought about it for weeks, looking at all these different tours offered by the company (they were called Xtreme Gap Year for those who are interested, and no I'm not affiliated). Kickboxing classes on a tropical island, dive master programs, adventures around Thailand. They all seemed so exiting, so different. In the end I knew this was something I wanted. So I made the scariest decision of my life. I signed up for a four-week backpacking adventure through Thailand.

Looking back, I'm not sure whether I left because I was running away from real life, or because I had suddenly realised that that didn't *have* to be my life. I like to think it was the latter.

Regardless of whether you identify with this story or not, I think it's important to think about your reasons for travelling. Why do you want to leave everything behind and see the world? Because despite what your Instagram feed would have you believe, travel is not the answer to all life's problems.

Yes, it's amazing, and I think everyone should have a chance to experience the world outside their comfort zone—and especially to travel by themselves at least once.

But at the end of the day, you still have to go home. And if you're not careful, you might just find yourself right back where you started.

If you *are* running away from something, that's okay—but just know that travel by itself won't fix what's broken. You also need something to run towards—a new goal or aspiration.

If you hate your job and decide to quit and travel the world, that's great! But take this time on the road to figure out what you really want to do, what excites you, what you're passionate about.

For myself, that meant pursuing my childhood dream of writing. During my first trip, I spent many afternoons polishing up an old fantasy manuscript I'd written during my university days. And at the end of 2015, I actually published it. Over the next four years, writing became not just my passion, but my career—and at the time of publishing this travel guide, I am the author of 12 fantasy and science fiction novels.

So that's my story.

Are you ready to write yours?

CHAPTER THREE

THE TERROR

So, you've had the push, you've started thinking about all the different places you might visit, the adventures you're going to have, the things you have to do before you go...

Oooh crap, that's a terrifying thought isn't it?

Leaving behind everyone and everything you've ever known and jumping on a plane to god-only-knows-what.

That's not just scary, that's *huge!*

Whoever you are, you're going to have to give up something. Maybe it's the career you've been working towards since graduating high school. Maybe it's the apartment you love, or the sports team you've been playing on for years. You're going to miss things—birthdays and anniversaries and reunions, maybe even weddings and the birth of new family members.

A loved one may pass away while you're overseas.

My grandmother developed cancer towards the end of my first trip. Fortunately, I was able to return home to say goodbye. Five years later, I was not as lucky when my second grandmother passed away while I was living in Buenos Aires.

Nothing really prepares you for that.

But if there's one thing I've learned over the years, it's that you cannot allow fear to dictate your decisions.

Solo travel can be scary.

Traveling solo forces you to face your fears.

Yes, sometimes you're going to be sad, or sick, or alone. There'll be times you long for the comforts of home. But you know what?

Solo travel is also exhilarating! While your friends and family are waiting back home, you get to jet off to new places and lands unknown, to have experiences they might only ever dream of. While your colleagues are getting in the car or taking the subway each day to work, you'll be rising early to start a jungle safari, or hiking the Andes in Peru, or skiing the Alps in Europe.

Travelling by yourself, without work or responsibilities to draw you back home, is the ultimate freedom.

I mean, think about it. In modern society, our entire lives could be depicted in a flow chart. We go to school, go to university, start a career, get a family, raise the kids, retire, die.

And I'm not saying there's anything actually wrong with that. We all make our own choices, and if I'm honest, there is a lot of comfort in routines, from receiving a regular pay check, in having a home.

But for you, right now, that doesn't *have* to be your life.

From the moment you quit your job, or book that one-way flight, or step off that plane, you're free.

Who knows where you'll be tomorrow, or next week, or next year?

Who knows who you'll meet, the experiences that await?

And you know what else?

Pictured: Freedom

Just because you're leaving, just because you've said goodbye to your friends and family and the "regular" way of life, it doesn't mean all that won't be there when you come back.

That was actually something my mother said to me the day I left. I was terrified. I'd never done anything like that before, flying off by myself. Heck, I don't even *like* flying! I'm afraid of falling, and something about being thousands of metres above the ground tends to niggle that fear. Yet here I was, heading off to Thailand with no one waiting to meet me and no idea what I was getting myself into. I didn't know if I could *actually do it*, if I was capable of surviving in this new environment.

So you know what my mother said to me?

"You can always come home."

Simple words, but they struck me to my core. Because at the end of the day, I wasn't really afraid of what was in front of me. What I was *really* afraid of was that I was giving something up, that by leaving everything behind, somehow things would never be the same.

And sure, *some* things will change. But your family will always love you. Your good friends will be there when you get back.

And home will always be waiting for you.

CHAPTER FOUR

TIME TO PACK

Phew, okay, enough of the mumbo jumbo, airy fairy stuff! If you've gotten this far, hopefully you're ready to make the leap and hit the road. So let's get down to the *real* stuff, shall we?

What are you going to pack?

Too much, I can almost guarantee it. Doesn't matter who you are, just about everyone I've ever met overpacked for their first solo trip—the singular exception being a woman I met in Istanbul.

She's actually the editor of this book, funny enough.

She managed to fit all her belongings into a 40L (medium size) backpack first try, which is a hell of a lot better than the 70L, 28kg (60 pounds) mammoth of a backpack I took with me to Thailand. Man, I shudder just thinking about it nowadays.

I guess I never quite realised that I *actually have to carry* all that stuff when I arrived. Cause that's the thing, right? You're on your own from the moment you step on that plane. And in the 30°C (86F), 100% humidity climate of Bangkok...well, let's just say it was a lesson well learnt.

Let's face it though, it's probably a lesson you're going to have to learn for yourself. I read any number of blogs and books before I left that said it was too much, yet I still did it.

To hell with it though, I'm going to give you some suggestions and tell you how I pack now, five years after that first venture out into the world.

For starters, my backpack is now a slim 28L and usually weighs around 10kg (22 pounds) in total. If you're interested in just exactly how big a difference that makes, well it's a good thing I took photos of my progress!

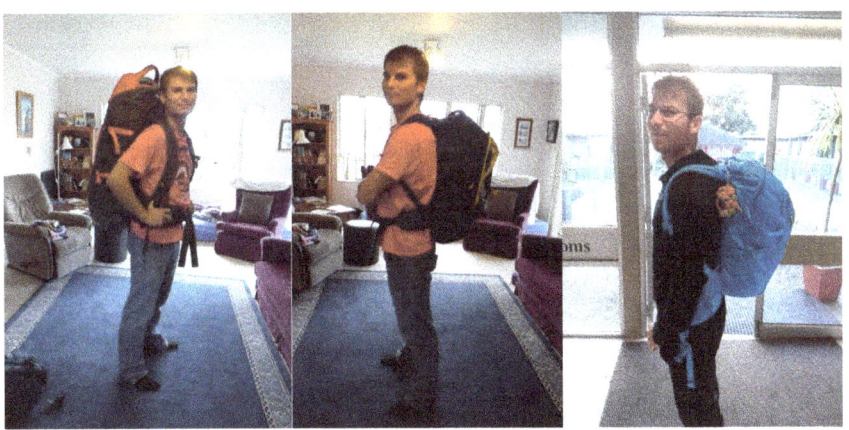

The evolution of a solo traveller

"Wow! That's amazing! I love you Aaron!"

Yes, those are all valid responses, but please wait until the end before asking for autographs…

Jokes aside, I still find it funny looking back at my 25-year-old self and wondering what the *hell* I was thinking bringing a sleeping bag and three pairs of pants and who remembers what else to Thailand.

Let me get that first one out of the way for you—unless you're going somewhere to do actual camping, and a lot of it, you're not going to need a sleeping bag.

Especially not in Thailand, where it's so hot you can hardly bear to sleep with a sheet. Plus, most accommodation providers will not let you use your own sleeping materials, as they can spread the infamous bedbugs! That goes for everywhere I've been except a few spots in Europe—which unsurprisingly is where I heard the most stories about bedbugs…

Anyway, let's start with what I brought on my last trip! Since I took a grand total of 18 months and went through Southeast Asia, India, Nepal, Europe, and North America, I can confidently say I experienced just about every climate you can imagine. And yes, I did all that with the 28L backpack you see above.

So, what was in my backpack?

THE ESSENTIALS

3-4 Packing cubes: These were a lifesaver when I discovered them. No more digging around in my bag for a clean t-shirt—with a few packing cubes I have all my clean shirts, pants, and shorts in one cube that I can easily pull out when I reach a new hostel.

Earplugs, eye shade, and neck pillow: You might be a deep sleeper, but eventually you're going to reach the end of your rope. Whether it's a night bus, a long flight, or that snorer who seems more animal than human, eventually you'll be longing for these comforts. I recommend getting them sooner rather than later!

Neck pillows are the best for long bus rides and flights!

Smartphone: This one might seem a bit obvious, but it's not exaggerating to say my smartphone has been a life saver over the years. On the road it's your map, translator, taxi, inflight movie, tour guide, and so much more. A few apps I recommend everyone install before leaving home are: Maps.Me (for the best offline maps), Google Translate, XE Currency Converter (with relevant currency rates preloaded), Hostelworld and Booking.com, Uber (or the local equivalent) and your local banking app (as you may not be able to install it overseas!)

Portable battery and spare charging cord: Considering the importance of your phone, running out of battery can be terrifying. I have a small 10,000mha battery that will do about two charges of my phone.

Waist money belt: *Not a money belt that goes over your clothes.* Seriously, those things are very easy to steal without your noticing. But a flat under-the-clothes money belt is useful for storing your passport, spare credit cards, and extra cash when in transit.

Multiple credit/debit cards: The easiest way to get local currency these days is by using your bank cards in the local ATMs. However, these important pieces of plastic are also very easy to lose—one way or a drunken other. The last thing you want is to have to resort to Western Union (it's expensive), so do yourself a favour. Bring a spare (or five), and keep them in different places in your luggage.

- PRO TIP: For those in the USA, a Charles Schwab debit card is essential—these charge no foreign transaction or ATM fees, and *will even refund* the fees of foreign ATMs.

Travel Insurance: I know some people will skip this, but it's really not worth the risk. And be sure you know exactly what your insurance covers—for instance, most companies will not cover items left unlocked in a dormitory as they count this as public space. You should also be aware of any restrictions to the type of activities that are covered by your policy. If you're going rock climbing or skiing or even riding a scooter, any accidents you have are unlikely to be covered by regular travel insurance. Trust me, a hospital bill in the thousands of dollars is a sure-fire way of ruining your trip!

Padlock: While many hostels now offer lockers in their dorm rooms, they often require you to have your own padlock to secure your valuables.

CLOTHING

4-6 t-shirts: The weight of clothing adds up quickly. I have mostly cotton clothing but if you can afford it, quick-dry and merino fabric will save you a lot of backpain!

2-3 shorts: For guys, at least one of these should be a swimsuit.

7-10 pairs of underwear: You might think that's *a lot* of underwear—especially compared to the rest of your clothes, but in a few months you'll come to realise the universal rule of backpacking—you only do laundry when you run out of underwear...

Swimsuit: For those who don't use a pair of shorts as their swimsuit.

1 pair of pants: Make sure they're lightweight so you can survive a night out in the steamy tropics! Black is the best colour to avoid those pesky stains after using them for two weeks straight.

1 jersey/hoodie/jumper: There seems to be a different name for this in every country, but at the end of the day, find something warmish that you can wear in those cold night buses (or you know, the mountains). I usually take a merino pullover that is lightweight but warm.

1 rain jacket: My favourite is a single layer Gore Tex jacket to keep dry in the tropical rain. They're also windproof, so when combined with thermals and a jersey, this will be enough to keep you warm in most climates!

Thermal clothing (top, bottom and undershirt): If you're thinking the above isn't going to keep you very warm in cooler climates, the trick is layers! Rather than taking bulky pants and jackets, a layer of thermal or merino underneath lighter clothing usually does the trick—unless you're someplace it's actually snowing!

You're not going to need a ski jacket unless it's actually snowing!

Flip flops and one pair of shoes: A pair of flip-flops is essential on the road, if only for the communal showers you'll likely be using! They also come in handy for the sweltering tropics, of course. As for a second pair of shoes, that's entirely up to your preferences and the climates you'll be visiting. For the tropics, I recommend either sneakers or hiking sandals—you'll be amazed at how hot your feet can get. For more mountainous destinations, a pair of hiking boots might be more appropriate. They also work great for cooler climates.

Portable washing line and universal plug with laundry powder: Depending on your destination, getting your laundry done can be very cheap (for example in SE Asia and Central America), or very expensive (*cough* Europe *cough*). Either way, these items can be useful for the odd bit of hand washing—for instance if you didn't pack enough underwear or want to stretch your supply of t-shirts out a few more days!

ALL-SORTS

Ziplock bags: Good for organising bits and pieces like cash, credit cards, toiletries, things for the bus—with the added bonus of keeping them dry should your bag get wet...which happens more often than you'd think. Remind me to tell you about the time someone in my room PEED ON MY BAG.

Toiletries: Don't pack everything under your sink. Seriously, most things from home can also be bought overseas. I usually take a couple 100ml bottles of shampoo (to be allowed as carry-on), soap, toothbrush, razor, and some deodorant (also don't be the person who sprays deodorant all over the dormitory!)

First aid kit: Depending on where you're going, you'll want common things like bandages and painkiller. You should also consider talking to a travel doctor about medicines for food poisoning, infections, etc.

Knife: Unless you're particularly handy, I wouldn't bother with a multitool or swiss army knife. The only parts I ever used from those was the actual knife, which I find handy for cutting up fruit, preparing meals in terrible hostel kitchens, and even opening coconuts. Downside is that you will have to check your bag at the airport.

Pack of cards: One of the best ways to bond with fellow travellers on the road!

Headlamp: Less necessary these days with phone flashlights, but still useful for hiking or reading at night in the more basic dormitories.

Camera/GoPro: Depending how good the camera on your phone is, one of these might not be necessary. Either way, be sure to take plenty of pictures on your trip. You'll regret not having them later, I promise you. Just be sure to also put the camera down afterwards and enjoy the sights with your own eyes.

Mask and snorkel: Personal preference this one, but I've often found the masks and snorkels available to rent are of a terrible quality. They often leak or fog up, which doesn't make for great snorkelling. I take my own personal dive mask whenever I'm in the tropics! I recommend one with tempered glass rather than cheap plastic.

E-reader: I only recently acquired this one, and have to say I love it. It's more lightweight and easier to pack than even a small book. Having said that, it can also be fun to discover new authors by using the book swaps provided at many hostels.

This was the contents of my backpack for my 2016 trip through Central and South America. As you can see, I still took too much!

OF COURSE, THAT'S MY PERSONAL PACKING LIST, AND AS A GUY there are probably some items I've missed that a female traveller wouldn't do without. For instance, many of the solo female travellers I've met also like to pack a few dresses. Not a problem! Just be sure they're light and easy-to-dry like the rest of your clothing.

Now, some of you might be thinking—wait, he travelled through Nepal, didn't he? And winter? Surely he couldn't have survived with so little clothing!

Well, technically you're right.

You see, I started off without any bulky winter clothing because I was planning to spend my first six months in Southeast Asia. And the temperatures there definitely do not require many warm clothes. A lightweight set of thermals, a jersey/hoody, pants and a rain jacket are more than sufficient, and they won't take up half your bag.

It wasn't until I reached Nepal that things got properly cold.

So you know what I did?

I took advantage of their lower prices to stock myself up for winter. A new pair of hiking boots, a heavy outer jacket, warm pants and socks and I was good to go. Not only did I avoid carrying all that gear for six months without using it, I actually got it all for less than I would have back home. I then had enough warm clothing to see me through the end of winter in Europe.

I've actually done this on all my trips—with ski gear in Canada, and hiking/winter clothes again while in Bolivia—and I cannot recommend it enough.

- PROTIP: If you're travelling to an expensive winter destination after a lengthy stint in warm climates, you can always have family ship your warm clothing rather than carry it around with you without using it.

Now for my biggest pet peeve I see on the road: travelling with jeans!

Arg.

Yeah I know they're easy and fashionable and all that, but for a lifestyle where you have to carry everything you own on your back, you know what else jeans are?

Heavy. Bulky. Impractical.

Not only do jeans weigh a tonne, not only do they take up a massive amount of space, but have you ever tried waiting for a pair to dry? Yeah, a literal eon.

No, a much more practical option, as mentioned in above, are pants made from quick-dry fabric. You can get these from most outdoor stores. They also have the bonus of being lightweight and cool enough to wear on those steamy tropical nights when you want to appear slightly classier than the average backpacker.

Lightweight hiking pants can keep the insects off in the jungle without the heat cooking you alive.

Okay, rant over.

Chances are you're going to ignore half of this advice anyway. You're going to do things your way, and bring things you don't need. Don't worry, I forgive you. And as with most things, it's not an irreversible mistake.

I'm embarrassed to admit it, but within a week of landing in Bangkok, I went to the post office and sent home a whole box load of crap. The sleeping bag, the extra warm clothes I didn't need, the heavy multitool. And over the next four months, I continued to throw things out or leave them behind as I realised I didn't need them.

However well you packed, there'll always be something you find you don't use. If it's tiny, like a needle and thread for mending clothes, maybe it's not a big deal. But if there's a pair of pants you never use, or a portable speaker that stopped working weeks ago, or a mosquito net you always THINK you're going use but never do, it might be time to ditch the extra weight.

Trust me, your back will thank you!

CHAPTER FIVE

FIRST STEPS

So, it's almost time to hit the road and join the ranks of solo travellers taking over the globe. But there's still just one question you need to answer before you go:

Where are you going?

Then again, the journey is the destination, so does it really matter where you're going?

OF COURSE.

Some places are *definitely* better for solo travellers than others—especially if this is your first real experience on the road. Where you decide to go is ultimately up to you, and while I'll be going over a few itineraries throughout the book, this chapter will give you a few things to consider before making your choice—as well as a little prep you should do before leaving on that jet plane.

The first thing you should ask yourself before choosing a destination is...where have you already been? For instance, Europe is a popular choice for many first timers—but if you're European, chances are you've already seen many of the highlights! Equally, if you grew up taking vacations in Cancun or the Caribbean, you might want to set your sights further afield.

That's not to say backpacking these destinations wouldn't be a completely different experience compared to a vacation, but it's more exciting if your first trip offers an entirely new experience. Plus, if you've already done a bit of travel you might be able to start higher up the "difficulty rating" of destinations (more on that shortly!).

Another thing to consider when choosing your destination is, somewhat strangely, your age. While I'm the first to say solo travel is for all ages, it's also easy to see that the age range of travellers varies wildly depending on where you go—especially when it comes to hostels. The Eastern European backpacker trail, for instance, (Berlin, Prague, Bratislava, Budapest, Belgrade) definitely play to the younger crowd, and more specifically the party scene. So if you're looking to let loose, this might be your crowd. If not, you might want to set your sights further afield!

Similar things can be said for backpackers in Southeast Asia, although depending on where you find yourself, the crowd may have a few more years under their belt. Compare this with South America, where language barriers and higher prices tend to require a more mature type of backpacker.

Depending on your personality and general sense of adventure, you might also want to consider how far off the beaten track you want to go. While it's always fun exploring new places—especially ones yet to be discovered by hordes of tourists—moving too far off the established routes can also be lonely. For instance, one of the most beautiful countries I've ever visited was Turkey. Travelling along the southern coast, seeing the ruins of Troy, visiting the Gallipoli peninsula (a very historically significant place for Kiwis), all of it was spectacular.

Every year on the 25th April, Kiwis and Australians come together and spend the night sleeping under the stars at Anzac Cove, Turkey, to commemorate the battle fought for the peninsula in World War I.

But it was also a bit quiet. There were very few hostels (something I'll be talking about in the next section), and even fewer travellers who spoke English. So wonderful as it was, after three weeks I was ready to take the ferry into Greece and make some new friends!

Other things you might want to consider when selecting a destination are your budget, time, and the types of activities you enjoy. South America tends to require more time and a bigger budget (although by no means does it need to break the bank) compared to a place like Southeast Asia where you can live like a king for a few bucks (might be a slight exaggeration). Language can also be an issue—you wouldn't believe the fright I got when I first showed up in Mexico City and realised almost no one spoke English!

After my experiences all over the world, I've actually now created a fun ranking system of the different regions. It is, of course, just a rough guide, and can still change drastically where you go in each country/region. But the ranking will at least give you some idea of the various difficulty of travelling in a few parts of the world, based on my own personal experiences. Level 1 = easiest, level 5 = hardest.

Level 1 (Europe, UK, USA, Canada, New Zealand, Australia): If you're reading this, you speak English, so you won't face a big language barrier in these places. They also generally have easily accessible public transport and a low level of crime. Plenty of hostels and other solo travellers to meet along the way.

Level 2 (Southeast Asia, parts of Eastern Europe, Turkey): While generally not the native language, there's still a lot of English speakers amongst the tourist industry. Pickpockets and petty crime may be more common, but generally still pretty safe. Transport might be more difficult or less comfortable, but can still often be booked online.

Transport in SE Asia tends to be less comfortable than Europe.

Level 3 (Mexico, South and Central America, Nepal): Language in these countries presents more of a problem. For instance, taxi drivers will now tell you the price in the local language. Transport options vary significantly (from comfortable and safe in Peru/Argentina, to hot and time-consuming in Central America). Safety definitely becomes a greater issue. I have personally never had any issues, but here you will meet fellow travellers who have been robbed/mugged/worse. With a greater degree of care it is still perfectly safe to travel here, though. This of course excludes countries that are currently experiencing political unrest or economic crashes such as Venezuela.

India is chaos personified. To reduce the stress of exploring this fascinating country, I recommend bringing a friend for this one.

Level 4 (India): Overwhelming, although this does vary significantly depending on where you are. Rajasthan is far more pleasant than Varanasi, while the south is more relaxed than the north. However, in general, India can be an overwhelming experience for a solo traveller. It has everything from air pollution, the noise of a thousand horns, absolute chaos in the streets, delicious food (poisoning), terrible (and good) intercity buses and trains, and more. Many, many people love their experience in India, but I would highly recommend bringing a buddy for this adventure. At the very least, you can share the stress of this strange and amazing country.

Level 5 (Parts of Africa and the Middle East?): You're waaaaay off the tourist track. Unexplored territory. I dunno man, I barely survived India! If you're travelling solo in a level 5, I'm impressed 😉

WELL, THAT'S MY RANKING SYSTEM ANYWAY.

For my money, I would recommend Southeast Asia for most first-time solo travellers. It has the best combination of cheap prices, amazing experiences, and difficulties that'll test your will to continue. It's far enough outside our western world that you're guaranteed to have an adventure, while still retaining enough infrastructure and a level of safety that means it's difficult to find yourself too far out of your depth. There's also a very lively backpacker scene, so you're unlikely to find yourself alone unless you go looking for it.

I'm also quite taken with the backpacker routes through Mexico and Central America—but fresh-faced new travellers may find they struggle a bit with the language barriers. And as it mentions in the charts, a slightly higher degree of caution is needed with your belongings and personal safety.

And finally, if all this has made you a bit nervous, don't be ashamed to start off with some kind of backpacker tour! As I mentioned earlier in this book, that's how I first hit the road. My first four weeks in Thailand with Xtreme Gap were actually amazing. I saw many places I doubt I would have visited without them. And the experience gave me the confidence to strike out on my own afterwards.

Just be sure it's a true backpacker tour with people your age—the last thing you want is to end up on yet another vacation with your parents!

CHAPTER SIX

BIG DECISIONS

So when it comes to travelling solo, there is one decision above all others that can really make or break the experience. And no, it's not your destination! We already talked about that, remember?

Your most important decision to make is where you're going to be sleeping!

There are all kinds of accommodation for the savvy traveller these days, from hotels, resorts, and hostels to Couchsurfing, Airbnb, and Workaway. All have their advantages and disadvantages, but for solo travellers I would eliminate hotels, Airbnbs and resorts almost straight away. While you'll probably get better sleep, none of these really have easy opportunities to interact with other guests.

And while that might be nice on occasion, it's also nice to have fellow travellers to share your travels and experiences with.

Yes, that means you're going to have to meet some people.

Of the remaining options, **a good hostel is far and away my favourite choice for accommodation.** Hostels are generally considered a place where the main style of accommodation are shared dormitories. They offer shared bathrooms and common spaces where you can meet other travellers. Obviously hostels aren't without their disadvantages. Yes, people snore and sometimes do…other things. But that's why you have your earplugs and eye shade, right?

In all seriousness, for a first time solo traveller, a good hostel is the best place to meet likeminded backpackers. Although I must emphasise the "good" part there. Not all hostels are made equal, and there've been more than a few times where I ended up in an empty dormitory—or worse.

Reviews are definitely your friend when first setting out. While there are many reservation sites, Hostelworld (hostelworld.com) is the best for most regions. It allows users to break down their review rankings into categories such as "cleanliness" and "atmosphere"—two ratings you're going to want to keep a close eye on!

The importance of cleanliness goes without saying. I've certainly found myself in some pretty filthy accommodation, but for the most part that's been when I chose accommodation outside of Hostelworld! The worst was easily an "inn" I stayed at in Kolkata, India. I won't go into the details, but let's just say I don't think the sheets or the toilets had ever been cleaned…

Aaanyway…

Atmosphere! As a solo traveller, this will be the most important rating for you. While it's by no means infallible, it does give you at least some indication of how sociable a hostel will be—meaning how likely you are to find other travellers looking to make friends.

The number of reviews can also give you an idea of the hostel's overall popularity, as you definitely don't want to end up in an empty hostel on your first day!

Modern hostels are often nicer than many budget hotels. This one is in Tulum, Mexico, and even offered a free Mezcal and Tequila tasting!

Other things to look for are whether their photos include guests of your age group, and if there are shared spaces where you'll be able to socialise with other travellers.

Some hostels even organise communal dinners where guests can get to know each other over a meal, before heading out together to see the local nightlife. Sadly, this practice isn't as common as I would like, but it's definitely something I keep an eye out for if I'm weighing up options between a few places!

If you're really lucky, the best hostels will run group activities each day for their guests. Surprisingly (because it doesn't generally have a big hostel culture), I found quite a few places in the United States that offered this service. My favourite was a day out kayaking on Lake Washington, organised by the Green Tortoise hostel in Seattle

The HI Hostel in San Francisco ran a bike tour over the Golden Gate Bridge and then returned us to the city via ferry.

—with a close second being a bike tour over the Golden Gate Bridge!

- PROTIP: Learn the difference between a party hostel versus asocial hostel. Travelling the world, you'll quickly learn the term "party hostel." To me, that term gets thrown around a little too generously as meaning a hostel that everyone drinks and goes out at night. Personally, I like to draw a line between true **party hostels** (where the entire focus of the hostel is getting drunk, partying and hooking up) and social hostels. **Social hostels** are still likely to have an element of drinking involved, but are more laid-back and focused around activities. As you become more experienced, you'll start to get a sense of the difference, and which of these hostels you prefer!

So that's hostels, more or less. Exciting, right?

Okay, don't stress, I know I said this was your most important decision, but it's also one you're going to be making again and again during your travels. So there's no point worrying too much about it. The more you explore, the more you'll learn how to spot a good hostel. Even better, you'll start to meet other travellers who can offer recommendations on where to stay in cities they've already visited.

That's my ultimate recommendation on how to choose a hostel, actually. **Above all else, personal recommendations are your best bet.** As you might imagine after reading everything above, it can be quite a challenge finding the best hostel based only on its website—and even then, you might still turn up and find it empty during low season. Compared with details on the internet, the advice of other travellers is almost always up-to-date.

And for some places, word of mouth is the *only* way they advertise. That's right—there are still some places that aren't listed on reservation sites! **gasp** In fact, the famous Los Amigos Hostel in Flores, Guatemala (okay, famous by backpacker standards) cannot be booked on either Hostelworld or Booking.com. Yet it is the most popular accommodation on the island, all just through the backpacker grapevine.

Pretty impressive, right?

Anyway, onwards! There were a few other accommodation types I mentioned at the start of this chapter—namely Couchsurfing (couchsurfing.com) and Workaway (workaway.com).

While I have not personally used Couchsurfing a lot, I know it is a popular way for travellers to visit more expensive regions such as Europe, Canada, USA, Australia and New Zealand. Couchsurfing is a website that allows hosts around the world to offer up their couch or spare bed to travellers for free. Its main advantages are that the accommodation is, well, free, and that you get a chance to meet locals. Most hosts at least want to interact with you a little or they wouldn't be doing it, and some will even go the full mile of showing you around the city. My cousin has travelled much of Europe this way, and a friend had the privilege of experiencing authentic Maori culture while staying with a host family in New Zealand.

However, Couchsurfing does require a lot of planning. The best hosts in the more popular and expensive cities are often booked up weeks or even months ahead of time, so you're going to be planning things a long way in advance. I usually prefer a more relaxed schedule so I can change my plans based on my experiences with places and people.

Then there is the issue of unreliable hosts. There were several times that my cousin's hosts cancelled their stay just a day or even hours before his arrival, leaving him stranded. While this was only a couple of instances over an entire year, it did end up a costly setback, as all the cheaper accommodation was already booked out.

And finally, there is obviously the issue of risk. This can be reduced by only staying with hosts who have plenty of good feedback—but at the end of the day you are still sleeping in a stranger's house, quite often on a communal couch. It's an experience I would recommend trying, but I wouldn't necessarily make it your primary type of accommodation.

Workaway (and other sites such as WOOF and HelpX) is similar to Couchsurfing in that you are usually staying with a local host, with the key difference being you'll be working for your food and bed! That's right—with a Workaway you will usually be working around twenty hours in a week (spread over 4-5 days) in exchange for a bed and meals.

Pictured: Some Workaways on the job at my house in Whakatane.

Again, the quality of your experience is going to change drastically based on your host. While I've never used this method of travel myself, my family has hosted numerous Workaway guests over the years. So I've heard a lot of their stories—everything from hosts who fed their guests spaghetti bolognese for a week straight, to those who would take their workers to the beach or for ice cream after a hard day's work. You'll definitely want to pay attention to the host's listing to know what type of work you're getting yourself into, and feedback is of course still important!

In general, I think work exchanges are more reliable than Couchsurfing and a more authentic way of getting to know locals than Airbnb. Most hosts are friendly and happy to have you there—because you're helping them in return. The bonus of having a meal as well as a bed also means you'll be saving even more money, as well as (hopefully) experiencing some of the local cuisine. They are certainly a good option for exploring more expensive locations!

My only warning is to be careful of hosts looking to take advantage of your labour. I've seen Workaways advertised asking for as much as 30 hours of work in exchange for a dormitory bed and free food—that somehow you still had to pay for! Even worse, this was in Colombia, where a hostel only costs 10USD a night.

You might also want to be aware of local employment laws. For instance, you might find hostels advertising for Workaways. In New Zealand, at least, this is dicey territory, as technically you should have a work visa and the "rewards" (bed/food) you receive from the hostel must be equivalent to what you would have made working those hours at the minimum wage.

Phew, okay, that's it! Remember, all of the above is only intended as a guideline. Hostels are still my favourite type of accommodation, but you'll quickly learn what your own preferences are when you hit the road.

Regardless of which you pick, after a few months of night buses and shared accommodation, you're going to be exhausted. So be sure to grab a private room or hotel every so often to catch up on your sleep and recharge the batteries.

Cause there's nothing worse than being sick in paradise!

CHAPTER SEVEN

GETTING THERE

So you've picked the destination and now you're ready to jet off on your adventure of a lifetime. Only problem is, how are you getting there!

Hopefully if you're going someplace exotic, you're going to have to take a flight. So the first step will be to book your tickets. This is your first test of how to be a savvy traveller—so let's not fail! The first thing you'll want to be exploring is how much the flight is going to stop and just how long it's going to take to get there.

Websites such as Google Flights (google.com/flights) and Skyscanner (skyscanner.net) should be your first stop for any trip. They allow you to not only see all the different airlines that fly your route, but also compare prices across a range of days so you don't accidentally end up flying on the most expensive day of the year. Even better than that, you can also compare the number of stopovers and total duration of the trip between airlines, meaning you can ultimately choose the best value flight in terms of time and money.

- PROTIP: The cheapest flights often do not include checked luggage—especially for short haul trips. You'll save a tonne of money over the duration of your trip if you can fit all your gear into a single backpack that is small enough to carry onboard.

Once you have your flight, its also a good idea to check up on the visa situation for the country you're visiting. What is a visa, you ask? That one's easy—a visa is basically a piece of paper or stamp that gives you permission to enter a country. Depending on what country you're from, this might be something you have to worry about for every place you visit. Or if you're lucky like me and from a country with a lot of visa waiver agreements, you will only have to worry about this on occasion.

Either way, it's still a good idea to check before you travel to any country whether you require a visa. The best resource I've found is the Wikipedia page Visa requirements by nationality. All you have to do is find your country in the list and it will give you the personal visa requirements of your citizenship in every country in the world.

The fine print on visas and visa waivers can also be pretty important. For instance, did you know that *most* countries require you to have proof of "onward travel" when you enter the country as a tourist? This means you may have to have a flight or bus ticket out of the country before you enter. Thankfully, countries that *actually* enforce this policy are pretty rare—to date the only ones

I've encountered are the United Kingdom, Panama, and Costa Rica.

However, if you're *flying* into the country, you still need to take onward travel into consideration. Because even though a country might not enforce the policy, many *airlines* will, because they are liable if you are refused entry (aka, they have to fly you back).

But what if you don't want to plan so far ahead in your trip, I hear you ask?

Good work, you're learning!

This is the exact problem many long-term travellers face, to the point where someone has created a website to solve this problem. For a 10USD fee, rentaticket.com/flyonward will book a legitimate exit ticket for you out of your destination country.

- PROTIP: A free alternative is to take advantage of Orbitz 24-hour free cancellation. Book a flight out of your destination country a few hours before your flight and then cancel it on arrival. However, be aware that not all flights on Orbitz have this free cancellation…and believe me, that can be an expensive mistake!

The final thing to consider before your flight is your health. As already mentioned, you should **definitely have travel insurance.** But another health item to consider is whether there are any diseases prevalent in the country you're visiting that you might want to protect yourself from. For instance, in my case I made sure to get the rabies vaccine before heading to Southeast Asia, since I am always interacting with animals. I also updated my tetanus and got the Hepatitis A/B vaccination. On my trip to South America, I got the Yellow Fever vaccination as it is actually required by many countries in this region. And on my latest trip, I had a measles booster, given its current resurgences around the world.

This is a pretty apt illustration of why I needed rabies shots.

CHAPTER EIGHT

THE ARRIVAL

So you made it! Congrats! For a while there I didn't think you would. Thought you might have given up and were reading this in the office behind your bosses back. But here you are in paradise, ready to hit the road and have an adventure—

Stop right there!

Arriving in a new city/country is the prime time for local scammers to take advantage of your naïve and trusting self. The number of people who will pay two, three, or even five times the usual price for a taxi from the airport in a new city is absolutely astounding—and that's just the tip of the iceberg. Depending where you are, there are far worse scams you can fall for.

So how do you avoid being taken for a ride (both figuratively and literally)?

Research and preparation.

The first thing I do when travelling to a new city is to install the app Maps.ME and download the offline map for the area. Maps.ME is an app that offers offline maps that will allow you to navigate a city by GPS, even without internet. It's also community based, so in backpacking hotspots you'll often find tips and local spots marked out by fellow travellers that you would never have found on Google. Using Maps.ME, you can mark the location of your hostel and the bus/train station or airport you'll be arriving in. That'll give you some perspective as to how much effort it's going to take to get to your bed for the night--whether you can walk or will need to take a taxi or public transport.

Public transport?!

That's right—the first thing any savvy traveller does when arriving in a new place is to jump on the local transport. Depending on where you are, this can be as simple as handing a bus driver

Pictured: My mum taking some local transport in Thailand.

money, or as complicated as getting yourself a local bus card. To know which you'll be facing, your best bet is to jump on the Wiki-Travel page (wikitravel.org) for whatever city you'll be arriving in.

WikiTravel is a great website that has everything a traveller needs to know about most popular destinations. Some of the important sections are "Getting In," "Getting Around," and "Getting Out," which usually include detailed descriptions of the various methods of transport available for reaching your relevant bus, train station, or airport. It even tells you the number of the airport buses and where the nearest vendor is to get a public transport card (when relevant). Some airports also have shuttle bus companies available that can be a good compromise between a taxi and public transit—and WikiTravel will usually describe where to find them.

If you DO decide to take a taxi, WikiTravel can also tell you what prices to expect. This is pretty important, because the old charge-tourists-through-the-nose scam is pretty much universal. In many countries (especially in Southeast Asia and South America), you might even find yourself approached by a "taxi driver" in the airport and asked if you need a ride. If you think you're going to get a good price from these guys...think again.

- PRO TIP: It's almost always a bad idea accept help from someone that just comes up to you in public. They are very likely to have ulterior motives and it can be difficult to see the angle of their scam until it's already too late. A better idea is to choose a random stranger and ask *them* for help! There are a few places that are the exception to this rule. Honestly, the people in Portland are *lovely*—I've never had so many people stop and offer to help me with directions! The same goes with New Zealand—if you're having car problems on the side of the road, it usually won't take long for someone to stop and see if you need a hand.

In most countries, when taking a taxi from the airport or bus/train station, you can follow the signs to an official taxi stand. Here you will *usually* get the correct price or a metered cab—although you might have to stand in line for a while. WikiTravel and Maps.Me can help you find these when there is no signage.

Of course, the invention of Uber (and similar apps) has been a godsend for the travelling community—but unfortunately many places either discourage or outright ban Uber drivers from picking up at airports. You'll also need an internet connection, so while these apps might be useful once you're set up in a place, they aren't the ultimate solution when first stepping foot in a country.

Google Maps is another godsend, with more and more cities incorporating their public transit options into the app itself. This means in many modern cities, all you have to do is enter your location and select the public transport option, and Google Maps will tell you exactly what buses and trains you need to take to get there.

Although you'll still need an internet connection to do it!

- PRO TIP: Look up the local transit options while you're waiting for your flight, then take a screenshot of the instructions in case there is no Wi-Fi when you arrive at your destination.

Another thing to be wary of when arriving in a new country is the official exchange rate. Often you're not going to have any of the local currency upon arrival, so the first thing on your list of things to do will be getting some. Unfortunately, exchange booths in airports are notoriously expensive and usually offer terrible rates.

For that reason, I generally prefer to use an ATM and withdraw the maximum amount (as New Zealand doesn't offer a feeless card). Most of the cash I'll put in my concealed waist money bag, and only about twenty dollars in my wallet. This lets me pay for food and taxis on the way to my hostel without pulling out big wads of cash.

- PROTIP: Some ATMs will ask if you want to convert the transaction into your local currency. **This will almost always end up being more expensive.** If in doubt, keep it in the local currency so that you get your bank's official conversion rate. If you've got time though, you can check the exchange rate they're using with your XE Currency app.

Away from the airport, you might find exchange places with better rates if you have any foreign currency—but in some countries you'll need to be cautious of not receiving fake bills.

Finally, once you've settled on a plan to get from your arrival point to the hostel, or on what will be your first stop in a country, I don't recommend changing those plans on the fly—especially if you're in a country you aren't familiar with.

What do I mean by this? Well, if you're planning on taking a public bus to your hostel, don't change to the tram that *looks* like it goes in the direction you want, unless you are really sure it actually does!

Still confused? Okay, let me give you a personal example of the time my friend Jon and I arrived in Costa Rica.

We were coming overland from a small town called San Juan del Sur in Nicaragua, and had left a little late to make it to our intended destination—Monteverde. So instead we were going to stop in the city of Liberia for the night, and then press on the next morning. However, when we got to the border, a woman that worked for the bus company told us not to worry, that they had a bus that would take us directly to the entrance of Monteverde!

Well...online I had read there was no direct bus into Monteverde from the Nicaraguan border. But this woman seemed so confident, I decided to ignore my instincts and trust her...

That was a mistake.

A few hours passed on the bus before we realised we'd passed the first road to Monteverde. We leapt up and went to talk to the driver, who informed us (as far as we could tell from his little English and our poor spanish) that he would drop us off at the next road into Monteverde, and another bus would take us the rest of the way.

We were...less than impressed.

But at this point we didn't have much choice, so another half hour later, we found ourselves standing on the side of the highway, in the middle of *nowhere*, looking at this gravel road that supposedly lead to Monteverde. A look on the map told us it was a mere 30km/18mi away—we were almost there, or so we thought. A good thing too, since the sun was beginning to set.

So there we were, waiting on the side of the road, thinking this bus is going to show up at any minute.

And waiting.

And waiting.

Finally we decided to walk up the road a little way and attempt to hitchhike with the odd car that drove past. Sadly, I think they all knew from our backpacks where we were heading—and that wasn't the route they were taking.

Getting desperate, Jon started using his international SIM card to call hostels in Monteverde to ask if one could send a taxi. Most were shocked we were on that road. Apparently, it was in the worst condition of the three leading to the town, so bad in fact it would take at well over an hour for a taxi to travel the 30km/18mi.

And it was not going to be cheap.

After waiting on the road for close to an hour, with the sun setting and each of us at the end of our ropes, a man appeared from a nearby house. He walked down to us, calm as day, and asked if we needed to get to Monteverde.

Of course we said yes!

The man smiled and said he could take us—for 60USD.

The bus we'd taken had cost about 8USD and most hostels were less than 10USD a night, so that was quite a bit of money for us at the time. We looked at the road, wondering whether the bus might yet show up and save us, but we both knew it was a lost cause by then. After a bit of negotiation, we got him down to 40USD, and he waved us to come up to the house.

There we loaded into a van that barely looked like it would make it out of the driveway, let alone the hour-long journey to Monteverde. But we were out of options. The man had disappeared into his house, but he soon returned with wife and son in tow. Apparently, this was to be a family outing!

So off we went through the darkness.

It didn't take long for us to realize that the van's suspension was long gone. Probably not a big deal for an average street, but the gravel road we'd found ourselves on was another story. I tell you, I've never been thrown around in a backseat like that. Without seatbelts, all we could do was hang onto our seats and pray it would soon be over. The strong stench of gasoline fumes leaking through what I can only presume was a hole in the exhaust only added to our misery.

Jon had started off the day feeling under the weather, and as we started up this mountain path, he quickly got worse. As San Juan del Sur had been a very tropical place, we were kitted out in our lightweight shirts and shorts, but we hadn't accounted for the elevation gain to Monteverde. By the time we reached the town, the temperature had plummeted and Jon was in a sorry state.

But finally the end was in sight, really this time.Thankfully, we knew one hostel had space for us from our earlier calls, and it was there our saviours finally dropped us off. By that point we were both beyond caring about the grumpy receptionist and extortionate 40USD per night price of a private room.

We were just happy to be alive.

Silver lining—the hostel had hot water, which after six weeks of cold showers, almost made the whole adventure worth it.

Almost.

CHAPTER NINE

THIS IS NOT A VACATION

So. Let's take a breath and slow down.

One of the big mistakes many first-time travellers make is trying to do everything they can as fast as possible. They'll cram a million things into every single day and changes cities every other day.

Sounds exhausting!

And most definitely unsustainable if you're travelling for more than a couple weeks.

On the road, you'll soon learn that while travelling is exciting and different and invigorating, it can also be draining! Sure, on a two-week vacation you might summon

Pictured: Me after trying to keep up with a new traveller.

the energy to jump off a long-haul flight and rush straight to the

Eiffel Tower, before spending an afternoon in the Louvre and hitting the Parisian bars for the night.

But try keeping that pace up for three months straight, and you'll soon find yourself burnt out and ready to drop.

The key here is to take a breath and remember you have all the time in the world.

So what if you stay a few extra nights in Paris? Not only will you maintain the will to live, you'll also have a chance to really get to know the city, maybe even get a glimpse into how the average local experiences the city.

The other half of the equation is not only to slow things down, but also to relax when it comes to booking things in advance. You might get a few flights at a cheaper price, but that has the drawback of locking you into a fixed plan.

In other words, it takes away your freedom.

Remember when I said that the best part about solo travel was the freedom?

Well guess what—if you have the next six months of buses and flights planned out, that's not freedom!

That's not to say you shouldn't plan anything. Sometimes it's good to have an end date for a particular region, especially if you have visa requirements that mean you have to leave anyway. But that doesn't mean you need every stop from start to finish planned out in advance.

While travelling, it's important to be able to adjust your plans. Sometimes you might simply learn about another place you'd like to add to your itinerary. For instance, during my trip down the west coast of the United States in 2015, I booked all my buses and accommodation in advance to get the cheaper prices, since the USD was very high compared to other currencies at the time.

Then I saw some pictures of Yosemite National Park.

The entire drive to Yosemite was simply stunning.

But I already had my night bus from San Francisco to Los Angeles booked…

Don't worry, it worked out in the end. A friend and I managed to rent a car in San Francisco and drive to Yosemite for the day, before driving through the night all the way to Los Angeles. It was one hell of a trip and I still lost the money I'd spent on the bus, but at least I got to see Yosemite!

If I could do it again though, I would have loved to spend a few nights there, maybe even do a bit of rock climbing.

But we live and we learn—or in this case, hopefully my story teaches *you* something.

Of course, sometimes it's not places but people who make us want to change our plans. One of the things I've learnt on my adventures is that it's the people you meet that make the trip, rather than the things you do. Because no matter how beautiful the beaches or mountains are, they'll always be better with good friends.

But if your plans are too rigid, you might find yourself missing out on that company. What if a new group of travellers you've just met is taking an amazing hike in the morning, but your rigid schedule means you have to leave tomorrow? Or if you make some new friends, only to discover they're heading to a city you already decided to skip?

Keeping your schedule as relaxed as possible means you'll be able to go with the flow when you meet other travellers, and hopefully have the time to develop some deeper connections.

Because while you're travelling alone, that doesn't mean you have to *be* alone!

Some of my best friends today are people I met and travelled with during my time abroad. And the only reason that's been possible is because we were each flexible enough to change our plans. A Belgium woman we met in South America even completely changed her trip to travel with myself and Jon. If she hadn't, she never would have experienced the wonder that is the Galapagos Islands—truly the most magical place I've ever visited.

A TRIP THROUGH SOUTHEAST ASIA

So this is definitely not a Lonely Planet book and I'm not going to provide in-depth details of every place in the world you can visit, but I can at least outline a few of the major backpacker routes that exist around the world. I've put the cities more or less in the order that makes the most sense to travel in. In most cases that's also how I travelled, but ah, not all of 'em. I was *all over the place* in my first trip. I've also added a couple of places I missed that I wish I'd visited!

Enjoy!

THAILAND

Bangkok: Pure chaos, Bangkok is the first stop for most travellers in SE Asia. I love this city second every second time I visit—every other time I go I hate it. It's that sort of place. Don't miss Kao San Road, the gigantic malls, the Chatuchak weekend market, or the temples. Don't bother with a tour and don't fall for the multitude of tuk tuk scams!

Koh Tao: The biggest scuba diving hub in SE Asia (and the world). Take a few days to grab your Open Water scuba license and enjoy the nice beaches and party atmosphere. Also some nice climbing here.

The Thai islands are to die for.

Koh Phangan: Takes the party atmosphere of Koh Tao and adds gasoline. Home of the Full Moon Party (and a bunch of other smaller parties throughout the month). You'll want to time your visit based on the party dates cause there's not a lot else to do here.

An all-night party on the beach, the Full Moon Party on Koh Phangan is something you have to do once. PRO TIP: don't do it twice...

Koh Phi Phi: A beautiful island on the west coast of Thailand—so you'll need to take a boat-bus-boat transfer to reach it from the islands above (which are in the east). It's gonna be a long night but Koh Phi Phi has some amazing beaches along with free fire dancing shows. Hire a kayak and take a trip to monkey beach—just don't get too close to the critters! Another good place for rock climbing, although with the tropical rains I missed out.

Chiang Mai: After the southern islands, the northern highlands of Thailand are a welcome change. Make sure you stay in the old centre of town (inside the medieval walls) to avoid the traffic and enjoy the peaceful atmosphere. This city offers some of the best food in Thailand if you ask me. The Sunday market in the centre has

The Elephant Nature Park has the best reputation for elephant encounters in Chiang Mai.

great food and most venders will give you reasonable prices without the need to barter. This is the centre of elephant tourism in Thailand, but be sure to choose an eco-friendly one. You can also zipline but take care to choose a safe company. Also a good place to take some Thai cooking classes!

Pai: A four-hour ride in a minivan from Chiang Mai. Many people drive this route on scooters but I do not recommend this unless you have experience—it's a difficult, windy road. Beautiful place, very much a hippy town, but there are some great white-water rafting operators and overnight jungle hikes where you'll stay in local villages.

CAMBODIA

Siem Reap: Angkor Wat. Need I say more? Also a great party town and there are so many temples you might need a few days to see it all. Can be reached by flying from most cities in Thailand.

Angkor Wat and its surrounding temples cannot be missed.

Phnom Penh: Cambodia is a country with a tragic past. To understand the people here, every visitor should visit the Killing Fields close by the capital to learn about the atrocities that were committed under the nose of the international community. You will cry.

Koh Rong (and other islands): Cambodia is changing quickly, and nowhere faster than the islands. When I first went in 2014, Koh Rong was the backpacker island and Koh Rong Sanloem was practically undeveloped. In 2017, I heard Koh Rong had become a resort island and Koh Rong Sanloem was now the place for backpackers. During my 2014 visit, these were islands to get drunk and get high. It's also possible to scuba dive but visibility is nothing like Koh Tao.

Kampot: This is a stop I didn't manage to make, but I've heard good things about the hostels and activities here. One hostel apparently has a actual waterpark attached—if it still exists during your visit you'll hear about it from other travellers, guaranteed.

LAOS

Four Thousand Islands: When I travelled SE Asia the first time, Seam Reap was my last stop before I took a bus up into Laos. If you take this route, take a photo of your receipt for the trip, as even though the tour company advertised everything included, they charged us for a second bus and the boat to the islands (well they attempted to, until I gave them a piece of my mind). The Four Thousand Islands are a long way from anywhere and I only recommend stopping here during high season—it was empty when I went. Some great kayaking where you can see pink river dolphins and the largest waterfall (by volume) in SE Asia.

Vientiene: Your first or last stop in Laos if you skip the Four Thousand Islands in the south. A pretty city with some nice temples and some really good restaurants, but otherwise this city is mostly for retired travellers and visa runners from Thailand. Don't stay long.

Vang Vieng: Another place that is changing rapidly. Back in the day this was the backpacker hotspot of Laos. The attraction was to hire inner tubes and float down the river, stopping at up to seven bars to drink and take drugs. Yep, bad idea, and after repeated deaths the government finally took action. The activity still exists but the bars are now limited. Still good fun though, and the town also offers some great adventure sports—including tubing through caves, kayaking down the river, and outdoor rock climbing.

Hiring a bike and traversing the busy streets of Vientiene can be fun, but it's not the biggest hub for travellers under 50!

Vang Vieng has adapted to the change in tourism and is now a great destination for outdoor activities.

Luang Prabang: A cute little city with a mountain temple in the centre. Has some magical waterfalls nearby that can't be missed. There's something about this town that's hard to describe, an authenticity that's missing in many parts of SE Asia nowadays.

VIETNAM

Hanoi (plus Sapa and Halong Bay): Hanoi can be reached by plane from Luang Prabang (*DON'T* take the 26 hour bus), but Vietnam can be done in either direction (i.e. start in Ho Chi Minh instead). City is chaos with many interesting museums and lots of party hostels, but the main attractions are the overnight trips you can take from here. Be careful which Halong Bay trip you book because many tours will not deliver on what they promise. I recommend getting recommendations from someone who's already been, or book through a trusted hostel. The two-day tour is amazing and not to be missed. Hiking the mountainous rice fields of Sapa is also a great experience. I recommend

Sapa in the north of Vietnam is an entirely different environment to what you'll encounter in the rest of Southeast Asia.

taking an overnight tour in which you stay with a local family, so you can really enjoy the countryside).

Pictured: Ha Long Bay. Enough said.

Hue: Cute little town with some cool ruins and temples to explore in the centre, along with displays of planes and vehicles from the Vietnam war. A good place to stop for a night or two on your way down the country.

Hoi An: One of my favourite places in Vietnam. Hire some bikes and ride through the countryside to the beach. Little temples are all through the town and you can take a day trip to a nearby mountain temple. Also has great nightlife with the cheapest beer you'll ever see. If it still exists, the Good And Cheap Bar offered all-you-can-drink spirits for 5USD a night!

Nha Trang: A lot of people skip this city, but we had a great experience with our little group. I spent a morning scuba diving and then went to a mud spa with the others. The nightlife can be a little rougher with more crime here than other places in Vietnam. Also has a great beach. The highlight was a day trip to the Vinpearl Water Park, which is an island park with waterslides, shows, a free arcade, and a mountain rollercoaster. Absolutely amazing with friends!

Remember: never say no to a new experience!

Dalat: A peaceful little town in the mountains. The main reason most people stop in Dalat is to go canyoning! Make sure you find a reliable company as your safety is in their hands—you'll be spending the day rappelling down waterfalls and jumping off cliffs!

Dalat may only be known for one thing, but that thing is AWESOME.

Ho Chi Minh: The more Americanised version of Hanoi, the traffic here is still crazy but there are more cars than motorbikes. A day trip to the Ho Chi Minh tunnels is well worth it, as is the delta. It's possible to take a boat from Ho Chi Minh to/from Phnom Penh (Cambodia)—just make sure you have the right visa for a land entrance!

CHAPTER TEN

ALONE ON THE ROAD

I KNOW. DESPITE EVERYTHING I SAID IN THE FIRST FEW CHAPTERS, IT sucks to be alone sometimes. No matter how used to your own company you become, there'll always be days when you feel lonely, or sorry for yourself, or even just sad.

But that's life.

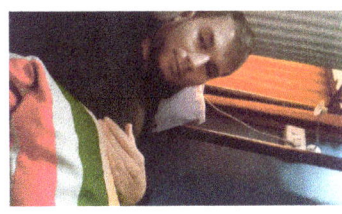

Travel isn't all fun and games. Being sick on the road really sucks.

Whether you're travelling, studying, or still stuck in that 9-to-5 job, there'll be times you feel down.

At least when you're travelling, you're someplace beautiful.

Well, except when you get sick. That really sucks being alone for. At least you won't have to drag yourself to work though, I guess?

In all seriousness though, one of my biggest concerns before I started travelling was that I would find myself alone for months on end. Thankfully, that fear turned out to be unfounded. You're never really alone while travelling—not unless you want to be.

Sure, you won't have your family or the friends you have known for years, but even that can be a blessing in disguise. Because the people you meet on the road don't know about your past, about your mistakes and heartbreaks; they only see the person you are today.

I know, that sounds a bit airy fairy, but it is true in many ways. Travelling by yourself gives you the freedom to become the person you want to be, to leave behind your past—or at least the parts you don't want to keep. Maybe it's not quite as simple as that, but you get the idea.

So embrace this new challenge and get out there and make some new friends. You never know who you're going to meet tomorrow.

BUT HOW CAN I MEET THE PEOPLES?

Woah, woah, calm down, I got you!

Remember how I talked about choosing the right hostel? Well, hopefully if you've followed my advice, you'll find yourself in a hostel full of fun, interesting people.

If this is *not* the case, or if your hostel is empty, I would recommend looking at others in the city and changing in the morning. While it can be nice having a dorm room to yourself, I usually prefer to have at least a little company!

Anyway, once you *do* have a hostel you're happy with, the job is mostly already done for you! All you have to do is say hi to the next person you see. After all, just about everyone else is in the exact same boat you are, and chances are they'll be just as happy as you to have someone to talk with!

Depending on the hostel, you might find people hanging out in the dorm room, or around the sofas, or over beers at a table or the hostel bar. Sometimes it can be a little intimidating walking up to a big group and saying hello. After all, they probably all know each other. You don't want to be that stranger who's intruding on their enjoyment...

Don't worry! This is a hostel, remember? Most of the people in that group you're afraid to approach probably only met a hot second ago. I guarantee you if you walk up and say hello they'll make you feel welcome.

Still nervous?

Okay, I'll tell you what. If your hostel has a bar, grab yourself a beer first. Once you've got that liquid courage in hand, go and say hello to someone.

Just do it! I swear they won't bite.

Of course, you won't always be lucky enough to find a group of people hanging out in your hostel. Sometimes people might be more focused on their phones, or perhaps everyone is busy running around doing tourist activities.

Regardless, this is one of the reasons why I really like hostels that offer group activities or communal dinners. They create a group atmosphere where people start talking and connecting. They also remove the need for you to take the initiative and approach other people.

Chicken!

Of course, you shouldn't be surprised if others come up to *you* and say hello. Or even invite you to join their group. As I said, everyone in a hostel is in the same boat. They want to make friends just as badly as you.

The longer you travel, the easier it is to cross that barrier and introduce yourself to fellow travellers. Before you know it, you'll be saying hello to everyone you encounter in your hostel.

You just have to take that first step.

CHAPTER ELEVEN

WHEN THINGS GO WRONG

Did I forget to mention this part?

That's right, **things are going to go wrong.**

And you know what? That's a good thing. If things aren't going wrong on your travels, that just means you're not taking any risks. And if you're not going to take any risks on this journey, what's the point?

It's kind of funny, but I've often had the Jim Carrey movie *Yes Man* in my head while travelling. It's the story about a man who decides he'll say yes to everything that comes along. Hilarity of course immediately ensues, but there is a lesson there.

We spend so much of our lives making excuses to *not* do something. It's amazing how many people tell me they wish they could travel the world—to which I say, what's stopping you? The answers are usually the same. Oh, but my job. Oh, but I don't have anyone to go with. Etc, etc, etc.

And yes, for some there truly are reasons travel is not possible. Health, family responsibilities, money issues.

Yet too often, we make excuses not because they are actual barriers to our goals, but because we're afraid of what will happen if we actually try. We're afraid we'll fail.

The fact is, I have met people from all walks of life on this journey. Entire families who have upended their lives and gone travelling with their kids, couples who decided to use their savings to hit the road and enjoy life, rather than continuing in jobs that were making them miserable. I've even met a retired couple in their 60s who were driving their campervan from Santiago, Chile, to New York, USA.

The difference is they didn't let excuses stop them. They didn't allow fear to rule their lives.

You can do the same.

Deciding to travel solo was the first step on the journey, but by no means the last.

What other risks are you going to take?

Just visiting some countries is a risk unto itself—although very much the kind that comes with so many positives that you'd be missing out to skip them. There are places in this world where even a simple bus ride can quickly turn into the adventure of a lifetime!

One of my favourite memories is of just such a bus ride in Mexico, between San Cristobal de las Casas and the town of Palenque. According to the bus schedule, this was meant to be a simple four-hour journey.

If only.

We were almost two hours into the trip and passing through a city when I decided to check on our progress. Pulling up my trusty Maps.Me app, I took a look at our location—only to discover we were on a *completely different route*. Several others in the bus realised this at the same time, and there was quite a bit of discussion in Spanish between the bus driver and my fellow passengers.

Not speaking any Spanish myself at the time, I had no idea what was going on.

Fortunately, at the time I was travelling with a Dutch guy who spoke some Spanish, and he was able to translate.

A teacher's protest had closed the main road between the two cities, so the bus was using an alternative route.

That was going to take eight hours.

Oh boy, I tell you, there weren't many happy faces on that bus. But there wasn't much we could do except sit back and accept our fate. Not being prepared for such a long ride, most of us didn't have much food or water, but we managed.

You'd think that would be the end of it, but I've found disasters rarely happen in isolation.

Around the seven-hour mark—now just one hour from Palenque—the bus came to a stop on the highway. There was a massive traffic jam and no one was going anywhere. We proceeded to sit there for half an hour before the bus *turned around and started driving backwards*.

At which point the whole bus erupted into shouting.

Fortunately we only drove backwards about a kilometre to where a second bus from the same company was *also* stuck in the traffic jam.

Sometimes a simple bus ride can turn into the adventure of a lifetime...

Our bus driver then proceeded to tell us (in Spanish) that there had been a big accident on the highway and they didn't know how long the road would be blocked. The second bus was going to head back the *seven hours to San Cristobal* and try the other road, while this one would continue to wait. We got to choose which bus we took.

Thinking a traffic jam couldn't *possibly* last seven hours, we decided to stay and wait.

Only problem was, the driver needed to turn off the bus to preserve fuel, so we lost the air conditioning that was keeping the 30C+(88F+) heat at bay.

Oh, and we were also starving and running desperately low on water.

Luckily, we'd spotted a little store up the road a way. With the bus going nowhere, my friend and I decided we'd go on a mission—as did roughly half the bus. On the walk we finally got talking to a few of our fellow travellers—a French Canadian woman and a couple from England.

The store was pretty much just the front of a woman's house, but it was reasonably well-stocked and we managed to refuel with some sandwiches and water.

That's when one of us had an idea that changed everything.

Tienes cervezas?

Si!

Well, that was that. Now stocked up with a dozen cans of beer, the five of us headed back to the bus. It must have been getting on six or seven in the evening by this time, so we were no longer directly in the sun—but it was still warm enough to be sweating. And the inside of the bus was worse.

While our fellow passengers crowded back into the sauna on wheels, we found ourselves a patch of grass on the side of the road and cracked open the beers. Someone had the idea to get a wireless speaker from their bag under the bus, along with a pack of cards, and soon the long wait no longer seemed like such a big deal.

Meanwhile, twenty other passengers continued to sit in the sweltering bus, determined to be miserable.

There might be a lesson there?

Some hours later, the five of us were pretty drunk and still having a good time, when we noticed a few cars were now driving past the long queue of trucks and buses. Thankfully, our new Canadian friend had been learning Spanish in Guatemala the last six months, and spoke well enough to ask our driver what was going on.

Apparently the police had opened up a tiny road for smaller vehicles to pass through.

We looked at the cars driving past.

Then at our 50-seat bus.

And insisted to the driver that we were in fact a small vehicle!

I don't know how we convinced him, but he actually went off and talked to a nearby policeman.

And suddenly we were all jumping back on the bus and setting off through the night!

An extremely bumpy drive down what can only be described as a farm road soon followed, with branches hitting the bus all the way. It was sometime around midnight by then, and drunk and exhausted I fell asleep—until suddenly we were in Palenque!

We were there!

Except we didn't have any accommodation booked…

Because we'd though we would arrive around 2pm, we'd been planning to take a taxi to the nearby jungle, where hostels that weren't available on the internet (at the time) could be found. But at one in the morning, that wasn't really an option anymore!

Fortunately, our new Canadian friend came to the rescue again. She had already organised to stay with a local Couchsurf, and had been in contact with the owner, who said it was okay for the other four of us to sleep the night on the floor.

Well, we weren't getting any other better offers at that time in the morning…

The Couchsurf certainly wasn't anything impressive—I think the woman was basically running a free hostel for travellers. There were people sleeping *everywhere*, in beds and hammocks and mattresses, along with the faint smell of animal faeces from the various cats and dogs wandering around. But by that time we weren't in any state to be fussy, and after finding a patch on the floor and laying down a few blankets the lady offered, we were soon fast asleep.

Five friends, our bonds forged in the fire of an 18 hour ordeal.

The next morning we rose with the sun, thanked the Couchsurf host for her hospitality, and set off in a taxi for the jungle village. There the five of us found ourselves a private room with five beds and proceeded to enjoy a *real* sleep, before spending the next few days exploring the ruins and waterfalls together.

It's interesting, how travel can pull and stretch you. Leaving your home country, travelling outside your normal world, it inevitably takes you beyond your comfort zone, tests you in a way life back home never will.

But that's a good thing, isn't it? It's only during adversity that we learn just what we're capable of, how much we've grown and learnt.

That story is still one of my favourite memories, even more than four years later. *Most* of the disasters that have befallen me are favourites, actually. So instead of freaking out the next time you're in the grips of a calamity, just think what a great story it's going to make one day.

Then just sit back, grab a beer, and enjoy the ride!

form
ADVENTURES IN MEXICO AND CENTRAL AMERICA

MEXICO

Mexico City: Most cheap flights into Mexico are for Mexico City or Cancun, so there's a good chance you'll start your trip here. There's a tonne to do too. Everything from going to a Lucha Libre wrestling match to visiting the nearby Teotihuacan pyramids. There are also tonnes of museums and interesting plazas to visit around the centre.

True story, I actually had no idea there were pyramids in Mexico. Especially not just a short bus ride out of Mexico City!

Oaxaca City: A few hours south of Mexico City, this town has a lot of colonial buildings to visit, along with churches and markets. There are also some impressive ruins close to the city. Perhaps the biggest attraction is Hierve el Agua, a stone waterfall with some crystal pools you can swim in.

Puerto Escondido: Here you'll find some of the most beautiful beaches in Mexico—with half the number of visitors as the Cancun region. A great place to learn how to surf if you don't already know, but also good for all levels of experience. Being a beach town, there's plenty of places to party. Only problem is to reach here you'll need to take a flight from Mexico City, or a very windy bus ride from Oaxaca City.

Puerto Escondido has some of the nicest beaches in Mexico.

San Cristobal de las Casas: An overnight bus ride from Puerto Escondido, this is another colonial city that's not to be missed. With a higher altitude, the cool nights are a nice break after the heat of Puerto Escondido. Nearby towns each offer different cultures and history and can be reached by local collective (minibus)—or by horse!

Palenque: Visiting the jungle ruins of Palenque is a fantastic experience. Surrounded by jungle, it's quite different from any of the other ruins I've seen in Mexico. It's worth the time to spend a few nights in the jungle itself—there's a few hostels and guesthouses you can stay in. You can also visit the beautiful Agua Azul Waterfalls.

Merida: Merida is a large city with a colonial area at its centre. The city itself is cute, but very hot, so make sure you find a place with a pool. The main attraction here is the nearby beach and the cenotes (massive stone sinkholes filled with freshwater). Take your swimsuit and enjoy a day tripping around the different cenotes and their crystal clear waters.

Isla Holbox: A more rustic (and cheaper and less crowded) version of Isla Mujeres near Cancun. If you're visiting at the right time of year this is the place to swim with whale sharks. Otherwise, there are still some great snorkelling tours from the island.

Cancun: The other main international airport in Mexico, but unless you're planning to spend some time in the resort, the faster you leave here the better.

Don't worry, Whale Sharks are vegetarians! These magnificent animals are generally found near Isla Holbox from June to September.

Playa Del Carmen: Party town to the extreme. Good for cheap drinks and a good time, but also has some diving that's worth trying—although I recommend going from Isla Cozumel for easier access to the nearby marine reserve.

LOOK AT THOSE THINGS! They're just begging to be eaten.

Isla Cozumel: Probably a good idea to avoid when the cruise ships are in port, but otherwise this island can be fairly laid back. Much bigger than Isla Holbox so you'll need to take a bus or taxi to visit the beaches on the other side of the island (which are beautiful). Some of the best diving in the world to be had here, with crystal clear waters and a marine reserve packed with turtles, stingrays, and lobsters the size of your arm!

Tulum: A cute little town further along the coast from Isla Cozumel. Great place to visit the local beaches, including one where turtles are so common you can take a mask and snorkel and simply swim off the beach to see them. The cenotes here are also much closer to town and can be reached via bicycle or a cheap taxi. I recommend Gran Cenote and Cenote Calavera for a day trip—especially if you combine them with the coastal ruins nearby. The jungle ruins of Coba are also nice to visit and are like a miniature version of Palenque.

Cenotes can be found all across the Yucutan Peninsula, but Gran Cenote near Tulum is one of the best.

Lake Bacalar: A small hippie town but not to be missed. Situated beside the crystal clear Lake Bacalar, it's a good place to spend a few days relaxing. Many hostels are right on the lakefront and run boat tours around the lake.

BELIZE

Caye Caulker: A tranquil Caribbean island just off the mainland of Belize. It is still the only place I've visited in Belize, but it's well worth the trip. If only it wasn't quite so stressful to get to.

What could be better than sailing the Caribbean? Unlimited rum on the way back!

If entering Belize from Mexico, you will almost certainly be charged an "exit fee" of around 20USD that you already paid when you flew into the country. Unfortunately, it's very difficult to argue with a border guard in the middle of nowhere. I was almost sent back to Mexico when I tried, so while I know people who've managed to avoid it, I recommend just counting this as part of the cost. If you want to save some money though, once you make it to Belize City, ignore the people offering boat rides/taxis at the bus station and walk the ten minutes to the docks. There you'll find Ocean Ferry Belize (just across the bridge) which has tickets to Caye Caulker for half the price of the more popular company.

On Caye Caulker itself you'll enjoy barbequed lobster for as little as 10USD. Do not miss the snorkel trip to the marine reserve on a yacht if you want to swim with sharks, turtles, stingrays and maybe even a manatee. I also took a spear fishing tour where we caught enough lobster and fish to make an awesome paella. The island itself has a relaxed nightlife.

What can I say, I like swimming with sharks!

GUATEMALA

Flores: Flores can be reached by booking a ticket directly from Caye Caulker (which includes the boat trip back to the mainland) or by booking a bus from the ferry terminal in Belize City. The only place to stay is Los Amigos Hostel, which you'll have to book through their website. Flores is a nice island town in the middle of a lake, but the main attraction are the nearby ruins of Tikal.

There are quite a few ancient ruins on this itinerary, but Tikal truly should not be missed. Pictured is just one of seven pyramids rising from a seemingly endless rainforest.

Semuc Champay: A series of beautiful crystal clear pools hidden in the middle of the jungle. A trip to Guatemala isn't complete without them—although they're a long bus ride from either direction. A tour through the water caves is also not to be missed.

Zephyr lodge is a local party hostel with an infinity pool high in the jungle. An alternative is to stay at the Utopia Eco Hotel/Hostel on the banks of the river, which allows you to hire inner tubes after your visit to the pools and float down the river back to Utopia.

Semuc Chumpay: Crystal clear pools fed by spring water, while below a river rages.

Lago de Atitlan: A massive lake surrounded by volcanos. Great place for hiking and kayaking. Each town is a little different. Panajachel is for more traditional tourists. San Pedro is for parties (although has a hippie flavour to it). San Marcos went full hippie. For something different, in Santa Cruz you can scuba dive the submerged hotels from twenty years ago. There's also plenty of hiking to do in this region.

Antigua: Probably one of the most popular places in the world to learn Spanish—and the cheapest. Lots of party hostels in this colonial city, but the thing you cannot miss is the overnight hike up Volcan Acetenango. Pick your weather right and you'll spend the night watching nearby Volcan Fuego erupting.

If you think watching Volcan Fuego erupt during the day is spectacular, wait until it gets dark.

El Paredon: This little beach town was made a destination a few years back by three Dutch backpackers who bought an old mansion and converted it into a hostel (The Driftwood Surfer).

Certainly a party hostel but also a beautiful black sand beach with plenty of surfing.

Rio Dulce: Not my favourite spot, but a worthy stop if you're on the way to Honduras. The Kangaroo Hostel is a hostel on an island in the middle of the river, which is a little different. I never took the manatee tour but apparently this is your best chance to see one of these strange creatures. My recommendation is to take a local collective to the hot water waterfall for a great day trip from the town.

Livingstone has some gorgeous scenery, but some less than clean beaches.

Livingstone: Accessible only by boat, this town is a few hours downriver from Rio Dulce. There's a few hostels right on the water again, which is nice, but it's nowhere near as impressive as Caye Caulker. However, from here you can catch the morning boat to Puerto Barrios and then pay for a shuttle all the way to Utila in Honduras!

HONDURAS

If you're taking the shuttle from Guatemala, be prepared for delays when you reach Honduras!

Utila: The main diving centre in Central America—especially for backpackers! Because most places charge in USD, their prices are a bit higher than a few years ago (when the USD was lower compared to other currencies), but they are still some of the best prices in the world.

The island itself is laid back with a chilled atmosphere, as everyone is there for the same thing: to learn to dive! Diving itself is better on the back side of the island where the water is clearer. If you missed them in Mexico, you can also occasionally see whale sharks here!

While there are other places in Honduras to visit, I don't know enough about them to comment as I caught another shuttle directly to Leon, Nicaragua.

Utila is a great place to do scuba courses. While there, I completed my certification to become a Rescue Diver. My graduation was everyone unexpectedly jumping off the boat and screaming for me to rescue them.

NICARAGUA

Note: When visiting Guatemala in 2018, I learned that Nicaragua is now almost empty of tourists due to the political protests at the time. However, there were still people traveling through, and at the time of writing this book, the situation was improving. If it's safe during your visit, I'd highly recommend going to Nicaragua, as its probably my second favourite Central American country

Leon: An old colonial city, Leon has plenty of history. It also has a nearby beach, although the waves are dangerous if you're not a confident swimmer. But the main reason to stop here is to go volcano surfing, which is about as crazy as it sounds.

Surprisingly, volcano boarding is exactly what it sounds like...

Granada: Another colonial town, Granada is set in the shadows of a nearby volcano. With beautiful old churches and plazas, it's well worth the visit. Take a boat ride on the lake to see the monkeys and other wildlife playing in the trees.

The twin island volcano of Ometepe is a lot larger than you think when reading about it. Make sure you leave enough time to get back to your accommodation before dark.

Ometepe: An island consisting of two volcanoes in the centre of Lake Nicaragua. Here you can find eco hotels in the middle of the forest, along with beaches and crystal clear springs for swimming. Buses travel around the island, or many people hire quad bikes to get around. For us, we managed to use the bus and hitchhiking.

San Juan Del Sur: San Juan Del Sur is the surf capital of Nicaragua and well worth the visit for the beautiful beaches and cheap surf lessons. It also once hosted Sunday Funday, a massive party hosted by several party hostels with pools. Personally, I skipped this one, but the idea was you paid around 20USD entrance fee and then spent the day with other guests partying your way through the three host hostels. With the drop in visitor numbers this may no longer be a thing though!

COSTA RICA

Monteverde: A town high in a mountain rainforest, complete with ziplining, night tours to see the local fauna, and plenty of hiking.

La Fortuna: La Fortuna can be reached from Monteverde by way of a bus-boat-bus service. Here you'll find a hot water stream in the jungle for swimming, as well as more fauna and waterfalls. There's also a very scenic volcano you can hike. Unfortunately, during my time here the clouds were so dense I never actually saw the volcano!

Puerto Viejo: I skipped San Jose and headed straight to Puerto Viejo by way of a whitewater rafting tour. This picked us up from La Fortuna and then delivered us to Puerto Viejo at the end. A little pricier than the direct tourist bus, but well worth the extra expense!

Puerto Viejo was easily the highlight of Costa Rica, with a free

Sloths are the best.

coastal national park just north of the town that was absolutely packed with wildlife.

The beaches south of the town could also be reached by bike, with sloths and monkeys and other animals so common here you'll literally see them on the side of the road and at the beaches.

You can get really close to the wildlife here. Like...really close.

PANAMA

Bocas del Toro: Bocas del Toro is a series of islands in the northeast of Panama. They can be reached pretty easily from Puerto Viejo by taking a bus to the border and a taxi the rest of the way (come with a group to keep the price low!).

The islands themselves have beaches and wildlife like Costa Rica (although not as much as Puerto Viejo), with the bonus of being a bit cheaper. There are various hostels on their own private beaches, along with several tours to beaches across the main island (Isla Colon) that are well worth the time.

Panama City: Not the most exciting city, but it is safe by comparison to other capital cities in Central America. And after a few months of backpacking it was nice to spend some time in a city with more modern facilities! The Panama Canal was…interesting, and probably not entirely worth the time and money. Grab some delicious ceviche from the shops at fisherman's wharf (you'll find all the locals here on the weekend as well). Casco Viejo is the historical part of town and is nice for a visit if you're not growing tired of colonial architecture.

BONUS: San Blas Islands: A popular way to get from Central America to South America is to take a yacht or speedboat from Panama through the San Blas Islands to Cartagena, Colombia. I've heard some people had a fantastic time doing this, while others were terribly seasick the entire time. Up to you whether you think the 550USD+ dollars is worth it. Alternatively, you can get a flight for as little as 80USD to many cities in Colombia.

I present the Panama Canal! There, you've seen it now, no need to waste your money on the entrance fee.

CHAPTER TWELVE

YOUR TRAVEL BLOG

Yeah...not gonna happen. Sorry.

CHAPTER THIRTEEN

CHANCE ENCOUNTERS

Some days I'm absolutely astounded by the different people I meet on my travels. Over the last four years, I've encountered travellers barely out of their teens who invested in cryptocurrency and made a fortune staying in the same hostels as former share traders and bankers who quit their corporate jobs to travel the world. I've met actors and actresses, former Hollywood casting directors, professional coaches for TED talks, and did I mention the retired couple driving their campervan through South America?

There was even this one guy who's been travelling for the last four years on the proceeds of his fantasy novels (okay that one's me).

All in all though, there are some general trends you'll start to see amongst travellers after some time on the road. The most general (and possibly most useful) classification is the age-old "tourists vs travellers" distinction. I tend to veer away from this topic usually, as I've noticed many travellers tend to get a holier-than-thou attitude about them when it comes to talking about tourists—as though they themselves aren't actually exactly that. There's even some who will go so far as to avoid popular attractions because they think they're too "touristy."

- PROTIP: Most places considered 'touristy' are popular for a reason! Yes, the Eiffel tower and the Taj Mahal get millions a year, but they're also *awesome* and absolutely should not be missed. A better idea is to find out what times are the busiest and do the opposite to avoid the worst of the crowds.

Just cause a million people have done something, doesn't mean you can't have fun doing it as well!

Ignoring the stereotypes thrown about, there is one distinction that can make it difficult for long-term travellers to befriend and travel with people on vacation—time.

Remember, as a traveller, you're in this for a *while*. There's no reason for you to speed your way through a country, doing and seeing everything in a matter of days. But that's not the case for everyone.

The average tourist only has a limited number of vacation days, so they're unlikely to be just putting their feet up at the hostel for a rest day. They need to be *doing* things—and then moving on to the next place!

And we've already discussed how exhausting *that* can be.

In other words, feel free to hang out with any tourists you meet on the road. Just like any other traveller, they have their stories to tell, they're interesting people, and it's always fun to hear about people's lives back home or in other countries.

Just be aware, it might not be a very long relationship!

But that's just another part of travel you'll soon come to understand—you get good at saying goodbye.

While it's true that there are always new people out there for you to meet, it's somewhat rarer to get to know someone well. You're constantly saying goodbye to people on the road, and in a way that's a good skill to learn.

However, this is also why you should keep your plans flexible. Because sometimes you're going to meet people who are really interesting, people you connect with, and on those occasions it's nice to have the opportunity to get to know them a little better.

I've already mentioned my friend Jon a few times, but I never told you how we met. It's the strangest story actually—an epic encounter involving everything from dirty laundry to the storm of the century.

It all started in Luang Prabang, Laos, where I vaguely remember some American guy saying hello to me at breakfast, before disappearing on a bus to Vang Vieng. Little did I know he was planning to return—he'd left all his clothes at a laundromat in town, so he didn't have much choice in that matter. Let's just say Jon is the king of travelling without a plan.

Anyway, I might have mentioned that things tend to go wrong on the road.

The night after Jon left Luang Prabang, the storm of all storms struck the country. We're talking torrential rain for 24 hours straight. By the next day, there was no running water in the city—and the only road between Luang Prabang and Vang Vieng was closed by no less than ten landslides.

Jon was not coming back by that route.

But he did have the contact details of an English guy who was still at our hostel in Luang Prabang. So Jon contacted him to ask where he was heading next. Upon learning the English guy was flying to Hanoi in a few days, they made plans for him to pick up Jon's laundry and meet up there.

It just so happened that Hanoi was also my next stop, along with several others in the hostel.

In the end, there were five of us who caught the same plane to Hanoi. Not having had any change of clothes for the last three days or so, Jon was pretty quick to meet us at the new hostel, where we all soon bonded over drinks and the delicious Vietnamese food. And more drinks…

Three Amigos in Vietnam.

Eventually (I'm talking days), we managed to sober up long enough to book a two night trip to the famous Halong Bay, and later a three day tour to the mountain village of Sapa. Along the way we lost the English guy who brought Jon's clothes, but he was replaced by an English woman who had also joined us on the flight from Luang Prabang. Along with myself and Jon, the three of us actually ended up travelling the entirety of Vietnam together—with several others we'd met around Hanoi dropping in and out of the picture.

All because of some lost laundry.

CHAPTER FOURTEEN

COUNTING PENNIES

Managing finances is perhaps the biggest concern for many first-time travellers—after all, you want to be able to keep up this new lifestyle for as long as possible, but you also don't want to be missing out on experiences for the sake of a few pennies.

Most new travellers tend to lean towards the latter in order to stretch their savings as far as possible. Which makes sense, as this might be the first time they've had to survive without any source of income. It's certainly important to draw a line between your previous lifestyle (whatever it might have been) and your new world of travel.

But there are plenty of ways to be thrifty without sacrificing too much in the way of comfort. Right from the get-go, choosing a hostel over a hotel is going to save you a lot. Yes, you'll have to share a room with between three and thirty other people (YUP), but we've already talked about all the fantastic benefits that come with hostel life.

Using Workaway for accommodation is going to save you even more—but does come with the sacrifice of your time. If you've got unlimited weeks or months in a country, Workaways can offer an excellent way to get to know the locals—but you should also do the math and work out exactly how much your twenty hours of work a week is saving you.

Nothing worse than working five hours a day to save 10USD on a hostel bed.

In fact, many of the topics we've already covered are also ways of saving money. Public transport over taxis is of course going to save you a lot of money in the long-run. Likewise, travelling slowly also has the added benefit of savings, because buses and trains are often a fraction of the price of a flight (and they also have the added bonus of seeing more of the countryside along the way).

Although that's not to say flights are always the more expensive option—it does pay to check. For instance, in Argentina, flights are often the same price or even cheaper than the buses!

Even just doing things yourself rather than taking a tour can offer massive savings. During our trip to the Galapagos Islands, my friends and I looked into a four-day cruise that would take us to two islands and a bunch of beautiful spots. The total price came in at 800USD per person.

For the trip of a lifetime, maybe that would have been a good price...but it only took a few minutes of research to discover that many of the locations the cruise would stop at could in fact be reached yourself, and for the massive cost of...nothing!

So instead of spending all our money on a cruise, we took our sweet time in the Galapagos, staying a total of two and a half weeks across three islands. In that time we saw everything the cruise had included and more—including stunning white sand beaches, scuba diving with hammerhead sharks (actually not included in the cruise!), snorkelling with turtles and sea lions and penguins, hiking volcanos, and biking backroads at sunset.

A trip to the Galapagos should not be missed and might be far more affordable than you think.

For all that we spent just 1100USD during over the 18 days we stayed (and that includes 250USD for the scuba diving). If you're interested in traveling to the Galapagos, it's important to note that we also spent another 100USD on the entrance visa and 300USD on return flights.

Having said all that, there is one type of tour that I absolutely *love*, and would recommend everyone try—free walking tours!

While they aren't *actually* free (the guides work for tips), they are a great way to really get to know a new city. The guides are usually pretty damn good because of the tipping system, and they are always full of local knowledge and advice. For that reason, I like to jump on a walking tour my first day in a new city so I can get the down-low on all the best spots.

Oh, and the tours also have the added bonus of *actually telling you about what you're looking at!* I can tell you, pyramids and temples and ruins all get boring eventually if you aren't learning anything about their history. But with a walking tour, there's always something new and interesting to learn while you're checking out all those famous landmarks.

I actually wish I'd discovered free walking tours sooner!

Another one of your biggest expenses on the road is going to be food. Travelling by yourself in all these unique places, it's very tempting to spend all your time eating out. And I'm not saying this is a bad idea! In some places cooking for yourself is just not worth it. For instance, the delicious food in Southeast Asia can cost as little as 1USD for street food, and even local restaurants are unlikely to be more than the 3-5USD range!

On the other hand, it does tend to get a little pricey eating out in places such as South America or Europe. While you might still find food cheaper in Italy or Argentina than a meal back home, it's unlikely to serve your budget very well to make a habit of it. Even in traditionally budget friendly regions such as Central America, you might find the higher prices in Costa Rica a little jarring.

Thankfully, these regions do tend to offer more kitchens within hostels, so budget-conscious travellers can cook their spaghetti bolognese.

Other money savers can be things as simple as hand-washing your laundry when you know you've got a few days in one place. Again, the value of this does vary from region to region. In Mexico you might find laundromats that'll clean your clothes for as little as a few dollars, while even hostels in the United States usually offer washing machines for a decent price. But in Europe, you could find yourself down ten euros for a bag of laundry—something that is going to quickly add up!

- PROTIP: If laundry day is coming up and you *really* hate handwashing, look for a local Airbnb that includes a washing machine. That way you can knock off your laundry and catch up on a bit of "you time" all at once.

Another great way to save money (or more accurately, *not waste money*) is to **make sure your phone plan is cancelled before travelling.** Quite possibly the worst invention in this world is roaming fees, and you'll rack 'em up quickly if you've got your data on in a foreign country. I've met people who have received bills of several hundred dollars in roaming fees.

Worst. Waste. Of. Money. Ever.

Do yourself a favour and make sure your phone is unlocked—meaning it can be used with any mobile provider. That way when you arrive in a new country, you can head to a phone store and grab yourself a local SIM. In many countries they literally give them away for free—all you have to do is buy a prepaid plan for the month. The most I've paid for a SIM is five euros, and most prepaid plans with a decent chunk of data are in the 10-20USD range.

Another thing to consider is cutting off your recurring expenses back home if you're going to be away a long time. Trust me, you don't want to be servicing your apartment or making car payments while you're on the road. I've been asked many times how I can afford to travel so much, but the truth is it's usually cheaper for me to be on the road than it is to live in my own country!

Which brings me to my next point—the true savings are in the destination. Whatever your budget, there's a place in this world for you. In a general sense, New Zealand, Australia, Western Europe, the United Kingdom, United States and Canada are all at the top of the scale when it comes to price, while South America falls somewhere in the middle. Below that, Central America is cheap, and most of Southeast Asia is *really* cheap.

But even then, Europe can still be done on a shoestring by Couchsurfing, while Southeast Asia...okay even living like a king there isn't going to set you back much. I swear I had two massages a week during my time there and never spend more than 1000USD in a month.

Regardless of whether you're travelling through North America or Europe or Southeast Asia, there are two things you shouldn't skimp on.

Number one: **don't skimp the locals.** Remember, you are a visitor in another person's country. They don't have to let you in—they are letting you visit not only because they want to share their wonderful country, but also because your money is helping to support their economy.

This is not to say that you should give your money to scammers. I don't believe in rewarding bad behaviour.

But I do believe in rewarding good behaviour. So if you've just had a fantastic free walking tour, please give a good tip to your guide. They might have loved showing you around, but this is also their job.

If it's customary to leave a tip in a restaurant, make sure you find out how much it is and leave it.

Even bartering can be problematic. While I one hundred percent encourage travellers to engage in this tradition where it is customary, it is also important to remember exactly how much you're bartering over. After all, is it *really* important that you get that extra $0.50 off those elephant pants you want?

Don't miss the Eifel Tower while in Paris. The cheapest ticket allows you to walk up to the first platform and then take the elevator to the second.

Because I promise you, that money means a lot more to the local than it means to you.

Number two: **don't skimp on the big stuff**. By this, I simply mean don't get so carried away with saving money that you miss out on something truly special. Remember, you are on the trip of a lifetime. You might never get the chance to come back to this place—so why are you eating canned spaghetti when a real Italian pasta at the restaurant on the corner might only be four euros?

So order that delicious Argentine steak.

Visit Machu Pichu, and the Galapagos, and the Eiffel Tower.

I guarantee you won't regret it.

BACKPACKING SOUTH AMERICA

COLOMBIA

Medellin: You may have heard of this city from the Netflix show "Narcos," but the history of Medellin is so much more than Pablo Escobar. Be sure to take a free walking tour here, although you might have to book in advance to get on the most popular one. A trip around the metro and up the

Gautape is stunning. Also I guess this is why travel agencies give you free tshirts!

cable car to the national park is also worth the visit. The nearby Guatapé is an absolute must—as is climbing the giant rock in the centre. Many people spend a night or two there, but it can also be reached for a day trip using public transport. Medellin is also a popular activity to see a football/soccer game.

Cartagena: Colombia is one country you should definitely be checking the price of flights rather than assuming the buses are cheaper. I got a last minute flight between Medellin and Cartagena for just 20USD. Overall, Cartagena was not my favourite place. The beach is packed with hawkers and massage people who harass you to use their services or buy their products. The colonial port nature of the town is nice to look at, but it doesn't take long to get to know this city.

Tayrona National Park is beautiful—and hot!

Santa Marta: The areas around Santa Marta are absolutely stunning and should not be missed. The mountain town of Minca is renown for its coffee tours, while Taganga is known for its diving (however it also has the worst reputation for theft). Most beautiful and precious of all, though, is the Tayrona National Park. Hike through the jungle to a beautiful beach where you can camp or sleep in a hammock for the night and swim, drink, and eat to your heart's content.

Salento: Another amazing place to visit, Salento is a tiny town in Colombia's coffee region. There are of course coffee tours here, but they also offer adventure activities such as mountain biking and horse riding. The biggest attraction are the mountain palm trees that line the Cocora Valley—just a short jeep ride away from Salento. You'll find the jeeps themselves waiting for you in the town centre.

Salento is a magical place. If not for the Easter holidays booking out all the accommodation in town, I would have loved to stay much longer.

Bogota: Sadly, I only spent a few days in Bogota, but the reviews on this one are mixed. Many only use it as a stopping off point into or out of the country, and the lack of a metro in a big city is certainly a point against it. However, as with all places, there is no harm in taking a closer look to see if you discover something different!

ECUADOR

Guayaquil: Not the biggest tourist destination in Ecuador, but it does have an interesting history and some nice places to visit around the city. This was one of the first places I did a free walking tour (run by a local hostel). Some of the highlights include the Iguana Plaza (where there are hundreds of iguanas just hanging out) and the local university where you can see Galapagos tortoises.

Montanita: A beach town just a little ways north of Guayaquil, it was once popular but may have waned after the earthquake and the murders of several tourists in 2016. You might want to check the situation before you visit, but it was a beautiful town and a cheap place to party and learn to surf.

The lizards are more than a little friendly in Guayaquil.

The Galapagos Islands: I could probably write a whole book on this one, but I'll try to keep it brief. Don't take a cruise unless it's a long one that visits the smaller islands. An expensive place, it pays to take a bit of food from the mainland (sealed only, since no fresh food is allowed in your luggage). If there are a few of you, I recommend not booking your accommodation in advance (except your first nights). There was an excess of accommodation when we visited, and with three of us, we managed to negotiate a stay in private rooms for between 10-15USD a night per person. It's also possible to knock a few dollars off tours and the speedboats between islands when booking for multiple people. The main islands have public buses that can save you an expensive taxi ride! Also, be aware that your biggest cost in the Galapagos is the flight and the island fee (100USD), so be sure to make the most of your visit and stay a while.

Playa Blanca on Isla Santa Cruz is stunning—and free to visit.

Isla Santa Cruz is the main island in the Galapagos, and the place you'll likely be flying into. Don't miss out on diving with hammerhead sharks at Gordon Rocks (although be aware this is a challenging dive). You can also access the stunning white sand beach of Tortuga Bay for free on this island. There is also Las Grietas, a crystal clear channel of water between volcanic rocks that can easily be reached by taxi.

On Isla Isabela, go snorkelling for free in the little lagoon/bay known as Concha de Perla. If you're lucky, you might see one of the local penguins, and you're more than likely to find the sea lions playing in the water around you. You can also hire a bike and ride to the Wall of Tears, a strange thing in itself, but the highlight is riding back at sunset—when the wild Galapagos tortoises come out to feed. Don't get too close—their beaks are sharp! For 40USD per person at the time of our visit, take a tour up to Cerro Negra and walk around the volcanic fields. There is also a snorkel tour through Los Tunneles—a collection of volcanic tunnels—although be aware it is very susceptible to weather and you might find yourself heading to a different location (without any chance of a refund!).

I tried to respect this guy's privacy. Instead he walked over and tried to eat me.

This guy was so excited to see us, we played around for literal hours together!

Isla San Cristobal was probably my favourite spot in the Galapagos, although perhaps that's because its where we spent the most time. Some hotels a little further back from the bay here go for as little as 10USD per person a night. Wander through the forest to the bay of Muelle Tijeretas, where baby sea lions can often be seen playing in the water—and you can join them. You can also take a public bus across the island to the Galapagos Tortoise Centre, before going the rest of the way by taxi to the beach of Puerto Chino to spend the rest of the day (and taking the bus back).

Quito: Quito is a cool city with some astounding architecture. There are several impressive churches and cathedrals to visit, along with a cable car that will take you up to a national park on top of the nearby mountains. Quito is also *very* close to the centre of the world, and there is a tower nearby the city to commemorate it! The old town has yet more colonial buildings, but is no less impressive for it.

Banos: Banos is the adventure capital of Ecuador. They have everything here, although one of my favourites was hiring a bike in the town and then riding down the valley stopping at various waterfalls and bridges along the way. There's also canyoning, bridge jumping, rock climbing and whitewater rafting—plus a cheap thermal bath in town to sage your aches and pains afterwards!

Banos is the home of the famous swing over the edge of the world.

The alpine environment at the Cajas National Park offers a stark contrast to the rest of Ecuador.

Cuenca: Cuenca is an interesting little city that makes a good stopping point on the way to Peru. While it doesn't have the most going on, the nearby Cajas National Park offers scenic alpine hiking that shouldn't be missed.

PERU

Mancora: Located in the north of Peru, the beach town of Mancora is the first stop for many travellers heading south from Ecuador. If you're looking for a party, look no further than the Loki Hostel. There's also surfing here, but there are better places, and the town's main advantage is as a stopping point before the long journey south.

Huanchaco: This is the town with real surfing, although getting this far south the water can be a bit cooler if you're visiting in the wrong season. There are also the Chan Chan ruins, the remnants of an ancient civilisation that predated the Incas.

The water was cold but the surfing was...hard work!

Huaraz: The hiking capital of Peru. Here you'll find yourself high in the mountains with some amazing hikes to choose from.

Laguna 69 is probably one of the best day hikes in the world (although the altitude is something else!) Then there is the Santa Cruz valley—a three- to four-day hike through a valley surrounded by towering mountain peaks. Guided trips aren't expensive and include a guide, food, most of your equipment, and most importantly, mules to carry your gear!

Laguna 69 is a day trip from Huaraz, and one hell of a hike with the altitude. But...well I'll let you judge whether it was worth it.

Lima: The capital city, I didn't spend much time here, but that's not to say you shouldn't! Highlights include paragliding straight off the coastal cliffs. The cliff top walk is also scenic, and its fancy malls can be a good place to stock up on any electronics you might be missing (I found myself a new GoPro case).

Ica (Huacachina): Four hours by bus from Lima, Ica is a tiny town built around an oasis. While you won't be swimming here, it is an amazing place surrounded by high sand dunes. Not to be missed are the buggy tours that will take you on a literal roller coaster ride through the sand dunes—then let you slide down them on boards provided by the guide.

Yeah, skip the flight to Cusco, take the bus so you can stop in Ica on the way. It's worth it.

Cusco: To get to Cusco you either need to take an 18-hour bus ride from Ica or fly direct from Lima. If the former, make sure you take a Cruz Del Sur—they're the safest and most comfortable bus company in the country. I was *horribly sick* in Cusco so I missed out on a lot, but the rainbow mountains tour was apparently beautiful. There are also a bunch of Incan ruins around Cusco to see, but of course you're there for the famous Machu Pichu.

I mean, a photo in front of Machu Pichu is pretty much mandatory for any trip through South America isn't it?

If you've booked months in advance the Inca Trail is supposed to be a truly unique trip to the famous ruins, but if not, the Jungle Tour is my personal recommendation. There are various versions run by different companies, but it's basically 2-3 days of biking, hiking, ziplining and rafting until you get to Aguas Calientes, the town in the valley below Machu Pichu. Alternatively, the cheapest route is a 15USD, 6 hour bus followed by a 3 hour walk up train tracks to reach Aguas Calientes. I personally do not recommend this, as the direct train takes 3 hours and cost around 70USD.

BOLIVIA

Copacabana: I ended up skipping Copacabana/Isla del Sol because I still had not recovered from my illness in Cusco. However, according to my friends who went, it was a much better alternative to the city of Puno in Peru, to the point I've actually removed Puno from this guide. This is a good place to relax after the chaos of Cusco, enjoy the crystal clear skies (and stars), and even swim in the high altitude lake Titicaca.

La Paz: La Paz is a pretty chaotic city and a lot more rustic than other capitals in South America. However, it still has plenty to offer, including an...unforgettable witches' market and the very original Lucha Libre de Cholitas—a version of traditional wrestling but involving Bolivian women in tradi-

The death road was stunning. The landscape changes completely over the four hour bike.

tional dress. You can also bike the Death Road from here, which despite its frightening name, is completed safely by thousands of tourists each year. So long as you are sensible, pick a company with good equipment and guides, and have some experience on a bike, you should be fine.

Yeah, he's a big boy. We would later go swimming with pink river dolphins in the same river...

Rurrenabaque: Enter the Amazon! Rurrenabaque is the entrance to the Amazon in Bolivia. I highly recommend taking a flight here from La Paz—the roads and buses in Bolivia are not safe. We were able to book a tour through a recommended agency in La Paz that included our flights and a two-night Pampas Tour (a trip down the river through the jungle) for the same price we would have paid booking the flight independently (around 200USD).

The town itself is cute with a good French bakery. There's also a full jungle tour that comes recommended. On the Pampas tour itself we saw crocodiles and birds and lizards and snake—we even swam with pink river dolphins!

Salar de Uyuni: Uyuni can also be reached by flight from La Paz —and yes, I recommend flying. Just Google "Bolivian bus crashes" if you don't believe me about the roads. The town of Uyuni itself is less than special. Almost no one stays here for more than a night, which means the restaurants are pretty terrible to say the least. Here you have two options—take a day tour of the salt flats (which are absolutely stunning), or take the three-day salt flats tour that ends in Chile. The Atacama Desert in Chile is apparently amazing, but I chose the one-day option. That left me back in Uyuni, where I took a night train south to the border of Argentina. If you decide on this option, make sure you book a first-class seat; it's still very cheap and has heating, which you're gonna need in this place!

The salt flats are great for creating optical illusions. This is still my favourite photo EVER.

ARGENTINA

Tilcara: Tilcara is a place less visited on the backpacker trail, but is all the more interesting because of it. The hostels here are basic and you'll find mostly Argentine visitors, but despite the language barrier I found them very friendly, even inviting me on several hikes. Don't miss the fantastic Rainbow Mountains here—a jeep will take you directly to the summit, making them more accessible than the ones in Cusco. There are also tiny villages to visit in this area, some without even a road to access them! If you've seen the salt flats in Uyuni, Bolivia, don't bother with the ones here.

Argentina's fourteen coloured mountains can be reached by taking a jeep from Tilcara.

Salta: If you went through Northern Chile instead of Argentina, you can enter Argentina here. Salta is the gateway to northern

Argentina and a nice city in itself. There are all sorts of outdoor activities to be had here. There's also a train that will take you to the clouds.

Real Argentine cowboys, or Gauchos, start young!

Cafayate: One of the best wine regions in Argentina, hire a bike and go for a ride through the vineyards—just be sure to make plenty of stops for tastings. There's also some incredible canyon formations in this area that should not be missed. The local villages have the occasional gaucho (Argentine cowboys) festival, one of which my friends and I stumbled onto while biking the vineyards! When they noticed the three of us in the crowd, we were even invited to participate in the tug of war and sack races they were having in the middle of the street.

Tafi de valle: A quiet village near several lakes, there wasn't an awful lot to do here in the winter. But there are several historical ruins in the area as well as outdoor activities in the summer!

Mendoza: One of my favourite cities in Argentina, Mendoza is another of the big wine regions of the country. The city is also the gateway to the Andes and Aconcagua (the highest peak in South America). Lots of outdoor activities such as rock climbing and whitewater rafting, and hikes that can be reached with a car.

Explore a slightly different side of Mendoza and visit the National Park of Aconcagua.

CHILE

Santiago: Santiago is a gorgeous city nestled between the mountains and the ocean—although both are a few hours away. You can take a bus through the Andes from Mendoza to reach the city, or many international flights arrive here. Hike Cerro San Cristobal, the mountain in the centre of the city, or for an easier challenge, check out Cerro Santa Lucia and its castle.

Take the gondola up Cerro San Cristobal in Santiago to reach viewpoints and the best hikes.

Valparaiso & Vina del Mar: Right next to each other on the coast, Vina del Mar is Chile's wine region, while Valparaiso boasts the traditional streets and buildings of colonial times. You can also learn to surf here on the nearby beaches.

Pucon: A cute town in the south, Pucon is Chile's adventure capital. You can do everything from hiking a snow-capped active volcano, to riding essentially a bodyboard down through river rapids. There's also horseback riding, skiing in the winter, and whitewater rafting. During downtime, the town's idyllic location on the edge of a lake also makes it the idea place to relax.

A popular hike will kit you out for snow and take you to the top of the volcano nearby Pucon, where you can stare down into the active crater.

ARGENTINA (AGAIN)

Bariloche: Back in Argentina, Bariloche can be reached by taking a bus from Pucon to San Martin de los Andes, then a second bus south to Bariloche. Another good place to ski in the winter, while in the summer there are hikes all through the surrounding mountains and lakes. There are even overnight hikes such as Laguna Negra where you can stay in a mountain Refugio (hut).

Ushuaia: The bottom of the world, Ushuaia is the stopping-off point to get to Antarctica—if you have money (it's *really* expensive). But there's still plenty to do here if not. The Tierra del Fuego National Park is located nearby with spectacular mountains, forests and rivers to visit. There's also boat

Spend a day in Ushuaia exploring the massive Tierra del Fuego national park.

tours to see sea lions and penguins, and even diving if you dare to brave the icy waters.

There's not many glaciers like this in the world—and they're getting fewer every year. Don't miss Perito Moreno in El Calafate.

El Calafate: Here you can see one of the most incredible glaciers in the world (Perito Moreno), or even walk on top of this giant mass of ice. You might also spend some time in the nearby town of El Chalten, where hikes all through the fantastic Patagonia mountains can be organised.

Buenos Aires: The starting and stopping point for many travellers through South America, Buenos Aires is a city that mixes flavours of Europe with the more traditional cultures of South America. Don't miss the fascinating stories and architecture of the Recoleta Cemetery, nor the colourful neighbourhood of La Boca. Sip coffee or beer in the neighbourhood of Palermo or sit in the park taking Mate, a native herbal drink adopted by the peoples of Argentina and Uruguay.

Buenos Aires is my current home—I could probably write an entire book just on Argentina.

BONUS: Iguazu Falls: Some of the most stunning waterfalls in the world, these can be reached by flight from Buenos Aires for a weekend trip. There is also a 24 hour bus, but I highly advise checking the flights before taking any buses in Argentina, as they are often the same price as the flights.

Much warmer than Buenos Aires and a stunning sight, the Iguazu Falls are a great break from the cold if you're visiting Argentina in winter!

CHAPTER FIFTEEN

KEEPING SAFE

Safety is a big concern for many travellers before they head off on their first trip. So I'll start this section off with something I've come to realise over the last five years on the road—the world is a safer place than we're led to believe.

Think about it.

For most of us, our only experience of countries other than our own is what we learn from the news. But media companies do not cover all news equally. They need to sell papers, or clicks, or earn subscribers, or whatever. And there's one sad fact about that —good news doesn't sell.

Or at least not as much as bad news.

Which means newspapers and television are biased towards reporting disasters, as opposed to the massive reduction in drug use in Portugal, or the huge fall in world hunger over the last 25 years. They'll report the murder of a tourist in Mexico or Thailand, and ignore the tens of millions who visited those countries without incident.

I even have a personal story about this. Back in 2015 I spent a week in Guatemala before heading directly back to New Zealand. And I had a wonderful time, but while I was there large protests erupted against the president for a corruption scandal.

I like to think I'm usually pretty aware about the political on-goings of the countries I visit, but in this case, I didn't even notice!

So you can imagine my surprise when the protests were all over the news when I got back home. From the viewpoint of my family, it looked like Guatemala was falling to pieces. Yet I still did not hesitate to go back three months later, because I had friends visiting the country and knew that what had been on the television did not represent the entire country.

This is not to say you should completely disregard what the news is telling you about a place. During the recent protests in Santiago (2019), one of my friends who was visiting *was* tear gassed. But another friend who went a month later (after the curfew had been lifted), experienced far less disturbance.

Some countries even simply have a bad reputation that might be long outdated. For instance, people are always surprised to learn I've visited Albania and Turkey, because they have this idea these are dangerous countries.

Well, the murder rate in Albania is lower than the United States.

And while Turkey did suffer a terrorist attack in 2016 that tragically killed 45 people, they were not alone. In the same time period, France, Belgium, the United Kingdom, and Spain all suffered similar tragedies. Yet it was only Turkey's tourist industry that collapsed.

Yet another habit we have is to think an entire country is dangerous because of problems that might only exist in a very limited region. For instance, there are still occasional problems in Turkey's capital, Ankara, and of course you wouldn't want to travel too close to the Syrian border, but for all the regions I visited, I never once felt unsafe or worried for my security.

Turkey is stunning.

A similar thing can be said for much of Central America. While countries such as Honduras and El Salvador suffer significant murder rates, you will find the vast majority of crime occurs in the capital cities of Central America. For this reason, most travellers avoid these cities in favour of smaller places through the region.

Travelling the world is not without risks. But just as you might lock your door and avoid bad neighbourhoods in your home countries, there are ways to minimise your risk.

For starters, the first thing you need to realise is that when it comes to petty theft, you're at a much greater risk from your fellow travellers than the locals.

Why's that you ask?

Because they have the opportunity. It's a simple numbers game. Your bag and items are going to be unattended in your room for a large percentage of your time on the road, and chances are at some point, someone in your dormitory is going to be less than honest.

It's a hard thing to learn, but since most petty theft is a crime of opportunity…let's just say I know a few backpackers who've had cash go missing from their bags when it was not secured.

- PROTIP: Always carry a padlock with you. Not all hostels provide lockers, and those that do often require you to have your own lock. Even in hostels without a locker, I recommend securing your values in the main compartment of your backpack with your padlock. A thief is much less likely to walk out with your entire bag as opposed to a wad of cash or camera.

This is not to say you shouldn't *trust* your roommates. You're going to need friends, after all. Just make an effort not to leave valuables—*especially* cash—out in the open in a hostel.

Another time when you are at a higher risk of losing valuables is when you're in transit between cities and countries—for the simple reason that during these times you have *all* your stuff. Wallet, phone, cash, camera, computer, *everything*.

Which means they're also available for someone to steal.

The first measure I take during these times is to secure my most valuable possessions in the waist money belt under my clothes. I'm talking passport, credit cards, and most of my cash. This way, even if I somehow lose my backpack, wallet, phone, etc, I won't be stranded without any means of saving myself.

Next, if you have a day bag alongside your primary backpack, I recommend putting all your bulkier items in the day bag—cameras, laptops, etc—and then carrying it with you on the bus, train, or plane. This means they'll never be far from your person, and even should you fall asleep, you can always loop your leg through the bag's strap to avoid it walking off while your eyes are closed.

Finally, you can secure the remaining items in your backpack with a trusty padlock. This is especially important when putting luggage under the bus, as less than savoury people will occasionally search through these bags while you are in transit. While a padlock on the zipper won't stop a determined search, it does at least act as a deterrent.

At all other times, I suggest keeping the majority of your cash and valuables in a locker or locked in your backpack at the hostel. Usually 20USD worth of local currency and a travel debit card are more than enough to survive during the day, and minimises the risk should the worst happen and you're robbed.

Which brings me to the thing most people are *actually* afraid will happen on the road—encountering a "real" thief.

First off, methods of theft do tend to vary depending on where you are. For instance, pickpocketing seems to be prevalent in parts of Europe, and also in Southeast Asia.

In fact, one of the very few times I've ever been robbed took place in Bangkok while I was on a public ferry. Two pickpockets were running a very slick operation, and when my friend and I stood up to get off the boat, they managed to insert themselves between us.

The first I noticed them was when the guy proceeded to get *very* close to me—we're talking his crotch pressing against my backside. This diverted all my attention, but in the packed crowd, it wasn't exactly *that* unusual. Fortunately, I have developed a somewhat paranoid habit of checking my pockets *constantly*, so before we even got close to disembarking, I put a hand in my pocket and realised my phone was missing.

The Thai version of a ferry.

I immediately turned back and looked at crotch guy, but he was wearing skinny jeans and there was clearly nothing in his pockets. So I looked over his head and the head of the woman behind him, and told my friend, "They have my phone!"

My friend immediately replied with a stroke of genius, "I'll call it!"

She proceeded to pull out her own phone and quite obviously start dialling my number.

Thunk!

My phone made a loud noise as it struck the wooden deck of the boat. Hearing it, I quickly crouched down and snatched it up from where it had landed beside the woman.

Honestly, I was so relieved that it wasn't until we'd disembarked and the boat had pulled away that I realised the two strangers had been working together. The guy had swiped the phone, then passed it off to the woman to hold. Very slick.

Obviously the lesson here is not to let random dudes stick

crotches where they don't belong...or let people into your personal space, if we're being less crude. Sadly we don't always have a choice in this matter, especially on crowded public transport of clubs. In these cases, all you can do is be aware of your possessions and keep an eye out for suspicious people.

Sadly, pickpocketing is not the only risk to your stuff. Another technique that's probably the most popular in Southeast Asia is the good old snatch and go. This ranges from someone snatching your phone or wallet or bag and running off with it, to the more involved motorcycle thieves.

Ho Chi Minh has a particular reputation for these guys, as the smaller streets often have no sidewalk. This means anything within reach of passing traffic is fair game for a motorcycle thief.

Sadly, I got to witness this first-hand one night out with friends. Three of us were walking down a street back to our hostel, when a motorcycle suddenly shot past. Walking on the curbside, I didn't really think anything of it—until my friend started running after him! Even then it didn't really click, and I was really confused for a couple of seconds.

Then my friend turned and screamed that they'd taken her wallet. Even with a wrist strap on the wallet and riding at full speed, the guy on the back of the motorbike had managed to snatch it out of her hand. They were gone within a second with no chance to catch them, and we were left standing there having no idea what to do.

To make matters worse, a few minutes later, we met two girls further down the street who'd had the same thing happen.

Definitely not fun. But at least none of us were hurt. I have heard stories of people being dragged by a handbag or backpack strap when these thefts go wrong—although take this with a grain of salt. I've never met anyone this has actually happened to, and stories tend to grow in magnitude when passed along the backpacker grapevine.

So how can you avoid this happening to you? Well, there'll always be a bit of risk from these guys, they're just too quick. But a good rule is if you're on the street in Southeast Asia, **your phone and wallet should be in your pocket**. If you need to use your phone, keep a good grip on it and watch out for people and traffic (this is actually good advice in most places; you never know when someone might try a snatch and run).

As for handbags, I generally recommend against them in Southeast Asia. But if you do have one, make sure the bag itself is hanging away from the road. If you're out with friends, have them walk on the roadside of you so there is no opportunity for them to snatch it.

Which finally brings us to the most frightening form of theft—mugging with a weapon.

Thankfully, these are also the rarest in my experience. I have personally never met anyone in Southeast Asia who has been robbed by someone with a knife or gun.

Sadly, I cannot say the same for Central and South America.

Before I go on, I'm going to point out that during almost two years of living and travelling in Latin America, **I have never been mugged.**

But as I said, I do know people who haven't been so lucky. For the most part, these have almost all occurred at night and with knives (I cannot recall any experiences involving guns).

This is not an uncommon problem in countries that combine unreliable policing, high levels of poverty, and easy access to weapons. Fortunately though, many of these places *are* trying to improve things. Colombia is a great example of this; over the last decade, they've introduced many social policies that have made the country much safer—everything from transforming dilapidating buildings into libraries, to reclaiming public spaces by turning them into parks and plazas for family activities. But until the threat is reduced to zero, there are a few things savvy travellers can do to protect themselves.

Sadly, almost all the stories told to me by fellow travellers begin with 'well I was really wasted', followed by 'I went off by myself'.

So if you're going out in a new city, try to make some friends in the hostel to go out with first. Let's face it: drinking is more fun with company anyway, and then you'll at least have people to keep an eye on you and your drinks. Have a pact between you that if you're going to disappear, you'll let each other know—and if you do decide to go home early, do not walk home alone if you have any doubts about your safety.

This goes for everyone.

At the end of the day, the only thing you should be concerned about during any robbery—your own personal safety. Your items can be replaced, especially if you took out travel insurance as I recommended. Your life is irreplaceable.

Which brings me to the uncomfortable topic of sexual assault, and especially the risks female travellers face on the road. I'll start off by saying I know many, many female backpackers who have safely travelled the world by themselves. You might also find it reassuring to know that most of these savvy women were never truly alone on the road—like I've been saying all along, they meet people, make friends, and travel together, just like everyone else.

I won't pretend to know everything my friends have been through. Many have told me of times when men have followed them, of times when they have been afraid. But the suggestions in this chapter are as much about keeping yourself safe as your possessions.

So yeah, bad things can happen on the road. But please don't let that scare you off travelling. Because bad things can happen anywhere. All we can do is take precautions to reduce our own risk.

At the end of the day, you should be okay if you use your street smarts.

CHAPTER SIXTEEN

DISCOVERING YOURSELF

So you've reached the end. You've travelled around the world and learned all about yourself. Some might say that you've...discovered yourself!

I know, I know, I said right at the start that I wouldn't go there! That this was just some marketing tactic by blogs and guidebooks and all your friends who've already gone overseas and won't stop telling you about how amazing it was...

But you know what? They're right.

I might have mentioned once or twice already how much travel helps you grow and change. The trials and stress you face help you to become a more rounded person—or at least more adaptable to this chaotic world.

But you know what else is true?

Those "changes" aren't necessarily permanent.

Travelling the world is not going to solve all your problems, no matter how much you might hope it will. Your anxiety won't just vanish because you hiked a magic volcano. Your broken heart won't mend because you swam with sharks. That whirlwind travel romance might not have been as real and life-changing as you might have thought under the Caribbean sun.

One day you're going to have to go home.

And before you know it, you'll be back at your desk, doing the 9-to-5. An ordinary life.

And you know what?

That's okay.

That's real life.

Travel is amazing and exciting and everything else they say it is, but it's also **not real life.** It's an escape, a break from the real world. It can't go on forever.

Take it from someone who's been on the road almost non-stop for five years.

You might become good at meeting new people and saying goodbye—but repeating the same conversations—where you're from, what are you doing, where are you going—with an endless stream of different faces eventually becomes exhausting.

You might gain a thousand friends on Facebook or Instagram—but you'll yearn for real, permanent connections.

Everything changes, and everything stays the same.

If you *really* want to take something permanent from your travels, I suggest you go back to that very first question I asked.

Why are you travelling? Why weren't you happy at home?

Because if you hated your job, that isn't going to change if after a year abroad you return to the same career, the same office, the same desk.

If you left because of a relationship, travel won't magically make you any less alone when you return to the real world.

But if you know what you are lacking, travel might just help you find your answer. A new passion, a new career, a new life—if you truly want one.

I left New Zealand in 2014 heartbroken and stuck in a career I no longer believed in. In short, I was pretty lost. And I have to say on that first trip I had no plan, no idea, other than I wanted to travel for as long and as far as I could.

I wanted to escape.

And if I'd continued that way, maybe that would have been it. Maybe I would have travelled until the money ran out and then returned home to my old career.

But in mid-2015, my grandmother fell ill with cancer and I cut short my trip to come home and be with my family. With my mother, we stayed with my grandmother until she slowly slipped from this world. And over that time, I picked up an old novel I'd written during high school and university.

And I started to rewrite it.

For three months I worked on turning the draft into something readable. During that time, my grandmother passed away. I will always treasure that extra time I had with her. And I will treasure the gift she gave me—the time to start something new.

In December 2015, I published my very first novel, "Stormwielder."

And I have been an author ever since.

Now when I travel the world, I am no longer running. I'm exploring new landscapes, learning new things, absorbing new ideas, and all of it becomes a part of my work.

The oldest of eight, my grandmother raised most of her siblings, then raised eight children of her own. This photo was taken before I went away on my first trip in 2014.

I have learned it's alright to be alone, but also to seek company in hard times. That you must know your own worth, or no one will ever value you for your awesomeness. That you must love yourself first, so when the right person comes along, you'll be ready.

Sorry, that got pretty sappy, didn't it?

Moving on!

This brings me to my very last point—home doesn't change.

This can be hard to accept after months on the road, after all the crazy stuff that's happened to you, the people you've met, after "discovering yourself."

But it's true. To you it may feel like a lifetime ago since you were home, but for your friends, nothing of import has really happened. Don't be surprised if they can't understand where you've been and what you've done, or what it meant to you. To many people, traveling long-term, traveling solo—they think it's just a glorified vacation. A constant stream of sunny beaches and photos on your Instagram feed.

Even now, those of you reading this who have yet to start your adventure probably think it's all garbage.

That's fine.

Now I dare you to take the leap.

Go solo.

Aaron Hodges was born in 1989 in the small town of Whakatane, New Zealand. He studied for five years at the University of Auckland, completing a Bachelors of Science in Biology and Geography, and a Masters of Environmental Engineering. After working as an environmental consultant for two years, he grew tired of office work and decided to quit his job in 2014 and travel the world. One year later, he published his first novel - Stormwielder - while in Guatemala. Since then, he has honed his writing skills while travelling through parts of SE Asia, India, North and South America, Turkey and Europe, and now has over a dozen works to his name.

Today his adventures continue. If you've enjoyed this guide, be sure to follow him on Facebook or Instagram for news of his latest exploits, or you can subscribe to his weekly fantasy newsletter at aaronhodges.co.nz/newsletter-signup.